# TRISTRAM SHANDY'S WORLD

*"It is not actions, but opinions concerning actions, which disturb men."*

*Epictetus*

(Sterne's motto for Volume I of *Tristram Shandy)*

# TRISTRAM SHANDY'S WORLD *Sterne's* *Philosophical Rhetoric*

BY JOHN TRAUGOTT

UNIVERSITY OF CALIFORNIA PRESS

BERKELEY AND LOS ANGELES 1954

*University of California Press*
*Berkeley and Los Angeles, California*
*Cambridge University Press*
*London, England*
COPYRIGHT, 1954, BY THE REGENTS OF THE UNIVERSITY OF CALIFORNIA
*Library of Congress Catalog Card No. 51–11223*
*Printed in the United States of America*
*Designed by Marion Jackson*

*To*
*B. H. BRONSON*

# PREFACE

IF "REASON serves but to sharpen our sensibilities," as Sterne insisted, that risible though serious proposition is a proper excuse for my reasoning on his book. The eighteenth century had a peculiar wisdom which sometimes offends the rather solemn critics of our time. Rigorous and authoritarian systemization is now the mode—a mode nearly antithetical to the urbane sensibilities of the Augustans whom Sterne emulated. In their mocking moods they liked to read Horace, Erasmus, Rabelais, and Cervantes, artists who could simultaneously and critically apprehend the trivial and the serious, the world's ways and its ideals. Our sensibilities are usually out of order for this sort of apprehension: we are unwilling to believe that anyone could find it necessary or useful to mock the very notions on which he founds his faith. Sterne, who did just this, is particularly difficult for us because he literally made himself a literary character. We think this accomplishment merely a fantastic's joke when we doubt what Sterne, who constantly read Shakespeare, assumed: that jibes and death explain one another in the skull of Yorick. And we forget that that son of a whore, Death, participated in all the excellent fopperies of the Sentimental Journey. The following study of *Tristram Shandy* was written only as a sort of guide for the sensibilities of Sterne's modern reader, a guide which suggests that a serious conception can inform bagatelle. If my reasoning in this essay at times reveals my participation in the analytical compulsiveness of the contemporary critical spirit, I shall hope that the reader will forgive me and reflect the more on Sterne's original genius.

I should like to thank Professor Bertrand H. Bronson, of the University of California, who rallied me in one way or another until I discovered that I had finished this study, and whose wit and discrimination first made me aware of certain controlling critical questions. To Professors Charles Muscatine, Harold Kelling, Benjamin Lehman, and Mark Schorer, of the University of California, and Leonard F. Dean, of the University of Connecticut, I am beholden for their interest and charity. My wife, Maureen Traugott, is, of course, implicated in this work in ways too complicated for my own comprehension. Certain members of the University of California Library staff, Mrs. Elizabeth Hoover, Mrs. Lydia Park, and Mrs. Margaret Uridge, constantly aided my study.

J. T.

# CONTENTS

ix

## • *Part Two*

### STERNE'S RHETORIC AS A SYSTEM OF COMMUNICATION

# INTRODUCTION

STERNE was not unwilling that his readers should make themselves uneasy while at his book; to this end he left, as he tells us, "so many openings for equivocal strictures." He has had his way. In nearly every opening some critic has taken a stand, but, usually, with nicely averted eyes. Nineteenth-century horror has given way to twentieth-century indulgence; Sterne survives both, and, indeed, in his perverse way takes increase from both. Yet many appreciative readers have understood *Tristram Shandy* as a comedy that is one vast rhetorical trap for the unwary. For it is a book that beckons us—is it with a sensible smile or a civil leer?—into indulgence in all the marginal vices: sentiment, affectation, presumption, pedantry, puerility, pruriency, and so on through the category of our human blemishes. What a piece of work is Man! Sterne says,—so equivocally compounded. But if Sterne's wit encourages the reader to a dallying with unscrupulous or dubious ideas and affections, including the love of fools and madmen, it also insists upon the reader's catching himself at his lapse. Once awakened, of course, one is already convicted of participation in certain impurities. As a later ironic rhetorican, Shaw, was to set logical traps for his reader's instruction, so Sterne plotted rhetorical snares which engage and reveal the affections. That his rhetoric remains vital though it is concerned ostensibly with such antique interests as Locke's philosophy, rhetorical forms, and odd scraps of recondite lore, only suggests to us what the eighteenth-century reader was willing to take on faith: the proposition that there are common springs of behavior that work men. Abnormal psychology was not an eighteenth-century interest.

Though some readers are easily arrided by the self-knowledge (albeit of a very mundane sort) so discovered, others have never forgiven Sterne and have had a sort of revenge: on the one hand he is a foul satyr, a disgrace to his collar, a whining hypocrite, a presumptuous and really unlearned (someone is always discovering a Sterne "borrowing") pedant; and on the other, a whimsical sentimentalist or, at best, a whimsical humorist. A nineteenth-century edition of *Tristram Shandy* was retitled *My Uncle Toby,* and *The Beauties of Sterne* is in the libraries. And his sensible heart, his Shandy humor, have in our day been enough commended.[1] Whether Sterne is to be censured or felicitated for his literary and real characters is a question vastly uninteresting today. Once honestly read, *Tristram* fascinates us not merely for its Toby but for its ironic relation of Toby to Walter, to ourselves, and to all the world. It is a book of relations, revealed through a rhetorical wit of paradox and dialectical[2] ingenuity. Like Walter a rhetorician, Sterne could find the mainsprings of our reactions, and he wrote his book, toward the end of his life, because mere social carping and scoffing and flouting—and understanding—were not enough for him. He was an artist, and for all his Augustan satire of system builders he could see the masks and coloring of personality in the system of relations that is the Shandy world.

The present essay proceeds with that conviction to an analysis of

---

[1]Several recent considerations of Sterne seem to have markedly interrupted the tradition of unsympathetic critical opinion concerning the man and his work. Wilbur L. Cross's definitive biography, *The Life and Times of Laurence Sterne* (new ed., 2 vols.; Yale Univ. Press, 1925), and James A. Work's scholarly annotations and sensitive introductory essay for his edition of *Tristram Shandy* (New York, Odyssey Press, 1940), have made recent criticism possible. D. W. Jefferson, " 'Tristram Shandy' and the Tradition of Learned Wit," *Essays in Criticism,* I (July, 1951), 225-248, shows Sterne's relation to the Augustans and their exemplars such as Rabelais; Samuel Monk's introduction to his edition of *Tristram Shandy* (New York, Rinehart, 1950) considers Sterne's calculated structure and calculated designs on the reader; W. B. C. Watkins' biographical study in *Perilous Balance: The Tragic Genius of Swift, Johnson, and Sterne* (Princeton Univ. Press, 1939) has rehabilitated the man Sterne as a serious and responsible artist; and Ernest Dilworth's *The Unsentimental Journey of Laurence Sterne* (New York, King's Crown Press, 1948) reconsiders usefully that pejorative word "sentimental" as it is usually applied to Sterne. See also the essays of B. H. Lehman, "Of Time, Personality, and the Author," in *Studies in the Comic* (Univ. Calif. Publ. English, Vol. VIII, No. 2, 1941, pp. 239 ff.), and Edwin Muir, "Laurence Sterne," in *Essays on Literature and Society* (London, Hogarth, 1949).

[2]The term "dialectic" I use throughout this essay not in its strictly logical sense, but to mean a method of evolving conceptions through the implied logic of conflicting opinions and narratives which pose questions and suggest answers.

his rhetorical method. For he was a rhetorician and not a "novelist." A critic looking at Sterne as a chapter in his history of the novel will find him a sad case of arrested development: neither the characters, though they are as "real" as any in literature, nor the action, though it is indeed sufficiently complicated, develops as other than an argumentative device of the opinionative Tristram. What does develop is a history of the reader's mind. The *argumentum ad hominem* was Sterne's device for revealing his perceptions. He argued to his readers, using their own responses as his illustrations. Just as he argued the cause of a worldly morality to his parishioners by exciting their sentiments, vexing them, and then pointing to their motives for those sentiments, so Tristram speaks as a preacher, arguing not for sentiment or cynicism or whimsicality, those supposedly Shandean touchstones, but for the recognition of their real influences in our pharisaical rationales. Writing, properly managed, our author seems to say, is warfare with the reader.

In every way, Sterne's rhetoric in *Tristram* sets the affections at war, and the forms of his rhetoric are a map of that conflict. My Uncle Toby is no more important than My Father, and My Father's systems are mad only north-northwest. Possibly every one of the Shandys is mad in some direction (except My Mother, and she is a universal blank), but they are mad because everyone, including My Mother, does service as a "voice" in Tristram's crisscrossed rhetorical demonstration of the history of the mind. Tobys and Walters understand one another when they understand the human need of organizing one's own associations and symbols into some meaningful pattern. Toby is not deluded by his scheme, for he knows that it is his scheme alone and he knows also his own fallibility. Ultimately, Walter too sees himself as a figure in his own drama, and though it is part of that drama to be elaborately at odds with the world, he too, in Sterne's words, rides his Hobby-Horse on the King's Highway. Evil for Sterne is not the wearing of a mask, but the assumption that Your Worship alone of all men is not wearing a mask. Sterne enjoyed pulling down masks, but only so that the wearer might not forget the accouterment. There is no disputing about Hobby-Horses, but there is disputing when one assumes that he is himself the only knight errant pricking on the plain. There is, says Sterne, a fair field of folk. Tristram makes plain that the schemes of men, from the Sorbonne doctors' disputation *in utero* to the Lockean rationale, may be seen in one vast scheme as necessary orderings of human experience according to a standard human nature.

Such is the argument of Sterne's rhetoric, that rhetoric which is the real form of *Tristram*. In this study the concern is primarily with Sterne's peculiar persuasion as it is discovered in certain definite and repetitious patterns. Though *Tristram Shandy* is a medley of vividly characterized "voices" colliding in fractured plot-sequences, of interrogations of the reader, of learned wit-play, and of seemingly vagrant associations, it has the consistent pattern of demonstrating by stratagems of apparent paradox and contrast probable human reactions to certain archetypal situations. It is argument, just as the sermons of Mr. Yorick are argument, and the stratagems through which probable reactions are displayed when overtly called into the reader's consciousness (as they always are) become a map of the actions of the mind. The forms of rhetorical argument as Sterne uses them, his ingenious wit which can turn any side of an argument, are ultimately important not as logical development, but as symbols of our thinking processes. Sterne's end is discovered in his technique. But what, the traditional critic of Sterne will say,[3] has form to do with the work of a man who never thought, much less punctuated a thought? This study suggests not only that Sterne thought, but also that he thought critically and philosophically; not only that he punctuated, but that he had a rather carefully developed punctuation. Both as a pulpit rhetorician and a profane one he was always concerned with form and its possibilities for statement.

In large part this essay discusses the peculiar significance he achieved by warping certain traditional materials: the philosophy of John Locke and the standard schemes, available in countless manuals, for rhetorical invention. Both materials served his invention, and he developed from both a formalization for his witty drama of warring affections or conceptions.

It was Locke's scheme in the *Essay concerning Human Understanding* to invade "that sanctuary of vanity and ignorance" the use of

---

[3]The traditional critic of Sterne has recently appeared in the person of F. R. Leavis, whose concern for tradition in *The Great Tradition* (London, Chatto & Windus, 1948) has caused him to consign Sterne to a footnote on page 2, in which he warns us against triflers. Sterne, says Mr. Leavis, was "irresponsible," "nasty," and "trifling." One purpose of the present study is to distinguish seriousness from solemnity, a distinction Mr. Leavis does not always make.

"vague and insignificant forms of speech"; this scheme Sterne perverts to a rhetorical formula for the invention of dramatic situations (which are always symbols of mental gymnastics) in *Tristram.* Part One is concerned with that artistic process. Whereas Locke would resolutely analyze all ideas and exactly determine the significations of words in order to reconcile necessarily isolated minds (necessarily, because mind is substance and therefore unknowable), Sterne's purpose is to demonstrate and describe the constant frustration of such analysis, the impossibility of determining meaning apart from a context of human situations. Using Locke's terminology and logic with a solemn mock-devotion, Sterne sets up an interplay of characters, in which his readers are implicated by traps of sentiment and logic, as a test of the philosopher's method. Exploiting Locke's own skepticism to a point where, as analytical method, even his limited rationalism is undermined, Tristram-Sterne invents the dramatic situations implicit in these conflicts of personal apprehension. Every invention tightens the knot for the reader. By such implicit opposition to Locke's rationalism, and by explicit ridicule, too, Sterne maintains the case for wit, rather than rational analysis, in discovering and communicating human motives. If, philosophically considered, wit is a kind of *discordia concors* (an occult association of ideas), it is the most comprehensive technique for establishing relations: if communication depends upon establishing the most comprehensive relations (since it cannot depend upon rationalistic determination of ideas), wit is its most effective technique. Such was Sterne's logic. By burlesquing and subverting the philosophical assumptions of Locke, who believed wit to be a positive evil, Sterne protests the moral value of wit.

Part Two examines the particular structures of Sterne's wit, his dialectical techniques, his private rhetoric. Since he insists upon the efficacy of rhetorical wit in exploring human motives, the inventions on any topic examine dialectically, by verbal forms of paradox and contrast, probable reactions. Moreover, by the agency of various techniques, often by being enticed into an unsavory train of logic, the reader is forced to participate in the rhetorical proofs. Having spread his lime and with the bird in hand, Tristram then examines the reader's motives in accepting those proofs. Rhetoric becomes the subject of rhetoric, and the ironic view so created is one method of contrast among many which Sterne's rhetoric develops as the defining form of his persuasion. Thus does Sterne write a history of the mind. The forms of rhetoric are themselves the demonstrations of that history. This rhetorical play with philosophical and rhetorical forms — this play which reveals motives and measures one affection against another in various situations —is Sterne's pathetic comedy. By it he demonstrates that, though they will not analyze ideas, Tobys and Walters may communicate; that the ultimate fact of moral philosophy is human nature itself; that the "true" shibboleths and "objective" definitions by which we live mirror unaccountably our passions; and (perhaps most important) that such moral antitheses as "delicacy" and "concupiscence" are, indeed and alas, sometimes one affection.

- *Part One*

DETERMINATE IDEAS

OF "TRISTRAM SHANDY":

STERNE'S USE OF THE

MATERIALS OF LOCKE'S

"ESSAY CONCERNING

HUMAN UNDERSTANDING"

# CHAPTER ONE · The Shandean Comic Vision of Locke's Philosophy

## 1. The Word
## "Philosophy"

ANY BENIGN reader of *Tristram Shandy* accustoms himself to his own role on-stage in adjusting the rigging with Tristram. "I beg the reader will assist me here, to wheel -off my uncle Toby's ordnance behind the scenes . . . and clear the theatre, *if possible* . . ." [6.29.455].* Impossible; the stage is never clear; the reader always finds himself viewing himself in character. How many personae are there? As many as the reader may care to discover. He discovers for one thing that even his sex is doubtful: "Madam," "Sir," "Your Worship." "Unmistrusting ignorance" may be shot from ambush "ten times a day . . . if nine times a day, Madam, had not served your purpose." The reader comes to believe in the hermaphroditic as well as the other doubtful qualities of his role. Sterne was a preacher and insisted that his parishioners doubt themselves and discover themselves as all the personifications of his sermons. Walter

---

*The Life and Opinions of Tristram Shandy, Gentleman,* ed. James A. Work, (New York, Odyssey Press, 1940), Vol. VI, chap. xxix, p. 455. All subsequent references are to this edition and will be noted as above.

3

Shandy congratulated the preacher on this rhetorical technique: "I like the sermon well, replied my father,—'tis dramatic . . ." [2.17.141]. Sterne knew that he had a vested interest in dramatic rhetoric, and this is why Tristram so often acknowledges the excellences of his own demonstrations in the jargon of the theater.* In his wry development of the philosophy of John Locke, Sterne discovered a dramatic formula for the endless rhetorical inventions which demonstrate his conception of reality. These opinions of Tristram Shandy bespeak a philosophy; and it is with this philosophical content of Sterne's dramatic rhetoric that we are now concerned.

To speak of "philosophy" in a resolutely nonlogical work such as *Tristram Shandy* is of course a strain. Obviously every artist works on some hypothesis, if we consider a peculiar selection of phenomenal data as a hypothesis. But the artist "proves" nothing: he can only persuade by making his images descriptive of his peculiar selection or ordering. Thus he may by the "force and vivacity of the impression" induce a sort of belief (as Hume describes belief) in his system. The philosopher, on the other hand, at least pretends to apply the abstract principles of logic to experience, and pretends also to shun pure description with all its references to vague tastes and sentiments. The artistic hypothesis is revealed, then, as concrete, intensive, and intuitive; the philosophic as abstract, extensive, and logical. But while such distinctions must be made if the sanity, prerogatives, and dignities of both the artist and the philosopher are to be preserved, sometimes the artist uses the philosopher to realize certain areas of being. Sterne thus uses Locke. Both he and Locke had a hypothesis of human communication, and Sterne chose to exhibit his by putting the logic of Locke's to the test of description in dramatic situations. Furthermore, they shared a passionate skepticism which started them worrying about communication in the first place.

Sterne chose a peculiar set of data. He chose creatures "heteroclite in all their declensions," pushed and swerved by *seemingly* casual ideas, creatures stalked by affections like Chastity, which, gentle enough usually, can become "ramping and roaring lions"—creatures, in short, determined in private and devious ways. Given this population, the world stands in need of an ingenious rationale. So far as Sterne could

---

*See below, chap. vii.

contrive an order for this world of his, he was, in the broad sense noted above, a philosophical artist. Yet he stands accused (he is always on trial) of creating exquisite tableaux in which meaning begins and ends with the niceness of the pictures. Even the nastiness is nice. Goldsmith's catechizing Chinaman received an evaluation of *Tristram Shandy* that is by now pretty much standard: "The author had nothing but the jest in view; no dull moral lurking beneath, nor ill-natured satire to sour the reader's good-humour; he wisely considered, that moral and humour at the same time were quite overdoing the business."[1] No one bothers today, as did Goldsmith, to add the extra force of irony to such criticism. But the sentence stands.

Now if there is a philosophic vision of order—and where there is order, morality must be—in *Tristram Shandy,* there is also an inevitable and just question: why does the vision of order not appear to many readers, some of them honest enough? A rhetorical question, this, which logically must hang by while there is a try at finding what philosophy means in the conception of Tristram's rhetoric. As we consider the difficulties of understanding the order of the book, the question may find an answer.

The reason's work in the proofs of philosophy is arduous and always frustrated *somewhere* in every system. If the display of gymnastics and machines used to clear a way is wondrous enough, the display itself becomes a proper subject for satire. But such display is *not* Sterne's primary reference; for involuted and exfoliated as they are in the wreathing, his jests on the snares of belief and philosophy, were they not part of a larger purpose, could scarcely supply the tension requisite for evoking a dramatic situation or realizing a character. *Scriblerus,* for example, a mere satire on systems, is small addition to the stock of humanity. *Tristram Shandy* uses philosophical snarls for more than a satire on systems; it uses them as a dramatic device displaying human motives and for creating a world of human relations. And satire verges into comedy when it begins to consider the inescapable human situation. "Everything in this world, said my father, is big with jest,—and has wit in it, and instruction too,—if we can but find it out" [5.32.393]. And so, too, at that inevitable *somewhere* of philosophical frustration, big with jest as the situation may be, lies a dramatic engine—if the

---

[1]For numbered notes, see pp. 153–162.

artist can but find it out. Now Locke, like all philosophers, had a vision
of order that satisfied a passion in him. And although *Tristram Shandy*
is not a slight and fantastical exegesis of Locke's *Essay,* it evolves on
the energy of the same passion of skepticism and comes alive with the
drama implicit in Locke's failure to find a convincing relation between
two worlds, real and ideal. Locke will have it—Berkeley, one of
Locke's best critics, will not have it—that there are two worlds. We can
know only our ideas, says Locke; we can never know the substantive
reality of existence exterior to our own minds. But even accepting
Locke's fundamental hypothesis, almost any careful reader is likely to
feel uneasy in considering Locke's paradox that there can be a "proof"
of *"unknowable"* substance and its primary qualities. Poets have always
found a quickening dolefulness in the reminder that we are here as on a
darkling plain; but an especially peculiar—in Sterne's consideration of
Locke a comic—sort of agitation arises when the fact is "proved" philosophically. Of course, while Sterne's talents were purely mundane, he
yet found in certain aspects of this so worried problem of world-splicing,
ideal to real, and the consequent problem of communicating ideas, as
these problems find form in the rationale of the *Essay,* a real energy.
Since the truth is, if the test of truth is ridicule, that Sterne's characters
are utterly limited to their human fallibility,—when they are set down
on Locke's ontological vast abrupt, the abysm between ideas and reality,
they perfectly display the worldly problem of Locke's *Essay.*[2]

From the traditional material of Locke's philosophy with a talent
fantastically original, he constructed an order. What follows, therefore,
is an attempt not to match lines from Locke with some from Sterne, but
to demonstrate Sterne's peculiar use of the formal elements of Locke's
philosophy.

## 2. *The Dilemma of Locke's Rationalism and Sterne's Dramatic Engine*

Locke's *Essay,* despite the professional plainness of the author, is not
wanting in the ambiguity that is useful for varying interpretations; the
particular interpretation used here, therefore, carries no authority
except that of *Tristram Shandy*. It seems to develop from and answer to
Sterne's references to Locke, and it seems to fit a critical scheme which

imports meaning to those references. Nothing heterodox, I believe, is involved in this interpretation; in fact, it is an interpretation of only certain aspects of the *Essay*. The emphasis given those aspects is, I think, not correspondent to that of the *Essay,* but the concern here is with *Tristram Shandy* and not with Locke.

As general guides to this discussion of Locke two propositions are useful. First, both Locke and Sterne found primary energy in reflection on learned trumpery and its utter success in the world. So annoying a spectacle led Locke to nearly twenty years of investigation of the origin and extent of human knowledge. His awful conception was no less than to banish error. Still, although he could not abide men of lore and although he wanted to smash the all-knowing who would have tribute of the blind, Locke was a genuinely humble man, and he conceived the *Essay* as a guide for sweet reasonableness. Secondly, where our knowledge of the secret nature of reality, of substance cognitive and noncognitive, is frustrated, both Locke and Sterne suggest a method for finding our way. Locke's is a rational system for comparing ideas and determining language. Sterne's is something else, but by developing the possibilities of confusion or absurdity in Locke's rational system Sterne has created a dramatic engine which controls situation and character. The characters are so made that, operating on Locke's premises, they completely foil his rational method for communication. And in the consequent isolation of personalities the vitality of situations is maintained by the comic gropings of those personalities for some sort of concourse. The excitement of *Tristram Shandy* lies not in its whimsical view of man's nature, but in its rhetorical demonstration that what is easily called odd, whimsical, and eccentric *must* be related to the basic motivations of Everyman; that the reader must know the difficulty not only in communication with foreign minds but also in discovering his own.

The final doctrine of sympathy or sentimentalism which Sterne offers us depends upon our ability to understand the relations of ideas and words as they appear in human situations; he had always emphasized the pathetic proof[3] in his sermons, but Locke in affording a dramatic situation based upon the isolation of minds gave a use for the pathetic or sentimental (though not in the word's modern invidious sense) that is artistically essential to the Shandean world of conception.

The dilemma of Locke's rationalism as it is developed from the implications of his skepticism should serve as a reference for the various future turns of this discussion. For this reason it is discussed now, before we turn to a consideration in detail of the other area of Sterne's involvement in Locke's theory, his passionate sympathy for Locke's view of the limits of knowledge, a view which offers Sterne, as it did the rest of the age, a cutting edge to hold against mystery mongers and system builders.[4]

To the first problem, then, the dilemma of Locke's rationalism and Sterne's use of it.

As he begins to invent his Uncle Toby, Tristram laments elaborately the pains of character drawing: If "the proposed emendation of that arch-critick," Momus, had taken place, he says, nothing more would have been wanted in order to have taken a man's character [1.23.74]. The proposed emendation was a window in the breast through which to look on the interior machinations of your subject. Certainly the interiors of both characters and readers (for they too are performers in this book) are offered to view so often that this display can only be described as the principal work of the book. But "interior" almost always means the odd but not abnormal ideas and affections of characters and readers as they are revealed in activity which is made part of a probable human situation. That is, ideas are never analyzed according to Locke's rational rubric, but are made part of a context which permits us to see what those ideas mean in terms of normal human activity. Of course, it is obvious that had Sterne followed Locke we might have had a sort of Scriblerean satire on eccentricity (though a feeble one), but no drama, no personalities. Locke suggested, merely by way of warning, the possibilities of the isolation of minds, and Sterne carried his suggestions logically as far as they would go.

This lack of access, one soul to another, was certainly a controlling fact of life for both Sterne and Locke; for Sterne, I say again, it served as a basis for dramatic and comic development; for Locke it was a principal torment urging him to develop his rational system for the analysis of ideas and language. Of course, among Walter, Toby, Trim, Slop, Mr. Shandy, and the Widow Wadman no determinate idea ever lodged at a time in any two breasts, or perhaps not even in one. Whole conversations are *performed* without a single participant's understanding or having the least desire to understand. After a prologue by Tristram on Locke's directions for the rational comparison of ideas, Walter and Toby are put on the scene to run an empirical test of the philosopher's method [3.40–41.237–241]. Walter in earnest preface to his mighty metaphysic of noses announces a rival scholar's "solution." Walter wants no more of Toby than a small gasp of metaphysical wonder. But, "replied my uncle Toby, shattering a conceptual world, 'Can noses be dissolved?' " (We later find that Toby's naïveté is prologue to Walter's more profound naïveté in arguing the scholastic quiddities of the being and reality of Slawkenbergius' stranger's nose.) One more "determinate" idea is dissipated into the Shandean air, untasted, uncompared. And the nocturnal terrors of Mr. and Mrs. Shandy's bed of council are well known [6.17–18.435–439]. Never an idea crossed the marital couch. Just so, the Widow Wadman must abandon language and engage her puissant eye to make Toby realize the possibility of breaching her fortifications [8.23–25.575–578]. And so it goes—or, rather, doesn't go.

Such a total want of rational correspondence, such a self-preserving instinct, on every hand, to follow a fixed set of ideas, such utter inharmony, Mr. J. B. Priestley has carefully observed,[5] "deal death to philosophies and sciences and all reasonable intercourse and call up a horrible vision of humanity as a set of puppets worked on the wires of a few instincts. A satirist, loathing his species, could have taken such tragi-comical little creatures, each in the separate mechanical box of his mind, and made out of them a scene or narrative that would have jangled the nerves of a dozen generations. Sterne, however, . . . preserves the balance by emphasising what we might call the kinship of his people. If the Shandies cannot share one another's thoughts, they can share one another's feelings . . . [We] would be rather taken aback at the bleak satire of the narrative . . . if the unity in feeling, the mutual trust and affection, of the Shandies were not so broadly and so often emphasised."

If any one form shapes Sterne's work, it must be his sense of contrast, not the contrast of the world's affairs with a devoutly held moral conception, as with Swift, but a sense that can discover exceptions to any proposition. Such a need of exhibiting the dubious could not but be debilitating to artistic energy were it not contained by a constant contrast to the indubitable reality of social sympathy. Where he has exploited the skeptical possibilities of Locke's *Essay* in order to demonstrate the intellectual isolation of the Shandy people, therefore, Sterne has contrasted their absolute sympathetic correspondence. And, indeed, one may doubt that they are in the end even intellectually isolated, since all the Hobby-Horses, though they often find expression in language that falls dead from the speaker's mouth, are yet understood. Are Walter's "thoughts," for example, his nonsense words? Or are they his passional needs to discover his life in rationally explicable systems? Toby *does* understand the latter.

Now Locke, as indeed everyone not an anchorite, understands that the first condition for communication is provided by the fact that we consider society among men as a real affair. Yet the very logic of his substrational hypothesis of substance [2.23.1–37]* forces him to conceive men as having, each of them, a little world apart, shut up, self-regarding, and inaccessible to the vision of other, similar, worlds [4.4.1–3]. For mind is substance [2.27.2], and if asked "what is substance," the ultimate generator of complex ideas, one would have to say, Locke almost sighs, "something, he knew not what" [2.32.2 *et passim*]. But substance, that I-know-not-what, is reality, and reality, therefore, is beyond the possibility of rational conception. Consequently the effects of mental substance, ideas, and affections as perceived can be communicated only by the happy circumstance that minds may be caused to think alike by an exactly determined language [3]. Even so, however, one mind can never hope to know how or why another may work. Hume's notion of the association of ideas through custom bridges this communicative gap, but Locke's system leaves it open.

Here, Locke's theory abysmally separates the individual from reality, including other individuals, and even himself should he forget his past ideas. Dr. Johnson might as well have booted the stone to rescue Locke as to refute Berkeley. It is Locke's doctrine that isolates the mind. "Since the mind, in all its thoughts and reasonings, hath no other immediate object but its own ideas, which it alone does or can contemplate, it is evident that our knowledge is only conversant about them" [4.1.1]. Is this not the very chimera that exercised Boswell and

---

*An *Essay concerning Human Understanding* (6th ed.), Bk. II, chap. 23, paragraphs 1–37. All subsequent references to the *Essay* will be noted in this style.

stimulated Johnson's foot? Now hear Berkeley defending common sense: "You talked often as if you thought I maintained the nonexistence of sensible things; whereas in truth no one can be more thoroughly assured of their existence than I am, and it is you who doubt: I should have said, positively deny it. . . . Remember the matter you [Lockeans] contend for is an unknown somewhat . . . which is quite stripped of all sensible qualities and can neither be perceived by sense, nor apprehended by the mind."[6] This to Lockeans. To consider this matter analytically in relation to mind would certainly be to leave *Tristram Shandy* far behind, but this much pertinent to the Shandys may be said: Locke's theory denies any communication by public, nonanalytic activity of minds. Locke does not entertain any contextual view of communication; without determinate ideas signified by definitive words man is simply a beast who wants discourse of reason. The mind has no public character; it is not manifest in mere patterns of action or language, and so is not in any respect open to other intelligences. Berkeley makes himself merry with Locke's conception of communication and asks the reader to consider the understanding between children prating of sugarplums.[7]

The privacy of mind under these conditions is the ultimate fact with which a theory of communication must deal. Locke establishes this early: "Man, though he have great variety of thoughts, and such from which others as well as himself might receive profit and delight, yet they are all within his own breast, invisible, and hidden from others, nor can of themselves be made to appear. The comfort and advantage of society not being to be had without communication of thoughts, it was necessary that man should find out some external sensible signs, whereby those invisible ideas which his thoughts are made up of might be made known to others." [3.2.1.]

Communication, then, can proceed under Locke's theory only if those sounds which are words are the marks of the ideas of the speaker, as they are clearly understood by him (and to understand a complex idea is always to be able to analyze it into simple ones), and if the respondent has exactly the same marks for the same ideas. Naturally, if the engaging of this communicative mechanism were dependent upon the mere coincidence that the same idea with the same word attached to it should appear simultaneously in two minds, the little candle which

Locke allows human reason to be could illuminate nothing save a self-consuming void, with the few accidental sparks of human correspondence only limning the wastes around.

But this is a possible, perhaps necessary, implication of the logic of Locke's theory. (Locke did not entertain it.) Even ignoring the difficulty in knowing under Locke's hypothesis of knowledge that there is a reality of objects in nature which the mind's ideas may signify, or of other minds which may have corresponding ideas, frustrations are inevitable, certainly, in any attempt to analyze all ideas, to make them, in Locke's terminology, "determinate," and in "comparing"—as is necessary—all ideas rationally in order to import meaning to them in predications. This process of "comparing" is rather technical [2.11.4–5, 4.1.1–2], and, as Sterne views it, not productive of more than one particular piece of intellectual traffic between the brothers Shandy [3.40.237]. Yet, for Locke, "sagacity," that ultimate attribute of the rational mind, becomes manifest only as the mind demonstrates its ability to find out the agreement or disagreement of its ideas [4.1.3; 4.17.2]. With this point, Locke throws maxims and syllogisms out of the rational man's *ars logica*. He proves his point by a syllogism: "If syllogisms must be taken for the only proper instrument of reason and means of knowledge; it will follow, that before Aristotle there was not one man that did or could know anything by reason. . . . But God has not been so sparing to men to make them barely two-legged creatures, and left it to Aristotle to make them rational." [4.17.4.] Syllogisms simply are not needed, and they tend to invest with an air of scholarly mystery the simple human act of thinking. For what is thinking but intuiting relations among our ideas? [4.2]. No formula is needed for intuition. Yet there is some complication in this intuition. Everyone knows by immediate comparison that a part is less than a whole; this is knowledge by simple intuition. But there are ideas so separated that we cannot (although we shall as refined angelic spirits) [3.11.23] find immediately their agreement or disagreement save by interposing other ideas to form a chain of comparisons [4.17.7–8]; this is knowledge by mediant intuitions—"as a man," says Locke, "by a yard finds two houses to be of the same length" [4.17.18]. Says Sterne:

The gift of ratiocination and making syllogisms,—I mean in man,—for in superior classes of beings, such as angels and spirits,—'tis all done, may it please your worships, as they tell me, by INTUITION . . . The gift of doing it as it should be, amongst us,—or the great and principal act of ratiocination in man, as logicians tell us, is the finding out the agreement or disagreement of two ideas one with another, by the intervention of a third; (called the *medius terminus*). . .

Had the same great reasoner [Locke] looked on, as my father illustrated his systems of noses, and observed my uncle Toby's deportment,—what great attention he gave to every word,—and as oft as he took his pipe from his mouth, with what wonderful seriousness he contemplated the length of it,—surveying it transversely as he held it betwixt his finger and his thumb,—then foreright,—then this way, and then that, in all its possible directions and foreshortenings,—he would have concluded my uncle Toby had got hold of the *medius terminus;* and was syllogizing and measuring with it the truth of each hypothesis of long noses, in order as my father laid them before him. This by the bye, was more than my father wanted,—his aim in all the pains he was at in these philosophic lectures,— was to enable my uncle Toby not to *discuss* [compare],—but *comprehend*—to *hold* the grains and scruples of learning,—not to *weigh* them.—My uncle Toby, as you will read in the next chapter, did neither the one or the other. [3.40.237– 238]

Had Toby stood prepared to work *medii termini* as fast as Walter could form his philosophical sentences, he would still have encountered some little difficulty in analyzing the radical material of Walter's ideas. Clearly something outside the rational Lockean system is proceeding at both ends of this correspondence. Yet both Toby and Walter are but settling into their proper natures, and that, says Aristotle in the *Rhetoric,* is pleasure. Part of the pleasure is, in fact, that each understands the other's pleasure. This is a way of communication that depends upon the public character of our activity, mental or physical, and depends not at all upon the analysis of ideas. Is it not possible that Walter's principal strokes are merely to put his brother's mind in a disposition of wonder while he goes through his routine? It must be possible, for Tristram says just that. This end of language is suggested by Berkeley when he rejects Locke's insistence that communication means solely the transference of determinate ideas.[8] Indeed, Locke's view of mind, which prohibits public concourse of various mental activities, seems inadequate to explain the facts of the Shandy world, facts which Sterne does not allow the reader to forget. Anyone willing to stay at the job of reading *Tristram Shandy,* provided he is not an anti-Shandean (for all such are advised by Tristram to abandon it, in chapter xxxvi of Volume III), cannot fail to perceive the intellectual inharmony among the Shandys and the world of conception Sterne creates to achieve order in this potential wasteland. A realization of this conception has incidentally value as biography, and is necessary if we wish to understand this book as an example of how traditional materials can be used by an original talent. Moreover, and perhaps more important, when we scrutinize a book so often passed down to readers with critical assurance of its chaos, a study of its formal elements should be a slight balancing of the critical account. And finally, the critic, by appreciating Sterne's formal conceptions, can speak with objective reference and not merely quiver or shudder as personal impressions become pleasure or pain or, even, pleasing pain.

Such is the formal content of the dilemma of Locke's rationalism with which Sterne has constructed one control for his comedy. It concerns at bottom, of course, one universal of existence: the will to communicate. With Locke's hypotheses Sterne obviously has wrought something that is not Locke.

## 3. Learned Bagatelle, Skepticism, and the Shandean World

In that psychological room where most men keep obvious muniments, Sterne stored oddments, and it is with this maggoty area of his conception, his sally against the gerund-grinding windmills of learning, that we are now concerned. Locke tells us (and tells us again and again throughout his *Essay)* that his philosophical quest to discover the limits of reason was stimulated by his dismay at the utter success in the world of learned quacks. Sterne shares this passionate skepticism, and it energizes his own conception. But while Tristram's incidental satire echoes so often Locke's flings at the lumberyards of learning, it is in the trivial satiric play with odd scraps of lore of his Augustan exemplars and the long tradition of learned satire* behind them that Sterne discovered a manner for turning his skeptical notions to creative account. Since we are not here concerned with influences per se, but with the more significant matter of an artist's original use of traditional materials, we shall try to understand the organic place of this bagatelle, this use of the most trifling trifles, in the comedy that is Sterne's world of conception. Bagatelle is traditional ornament to the mask of the professional fool—a figure, Sterne reminds us, formerly honored, now unemployed.

---

*See note 1 to the Introduction, above.

And Tristram Shandy is an atavistic original showing the ancient leer of the professional fool. Like Montaigne and Rabelais, like Burton, like the Scriblerians, like Walter Shandy, Sterne was a snapper-up of considerable trifles, and in a mask of as subtle modality as that of Erasmus' Folly he spoke his mind. Like Walter he had a "thousand little sceptical notions of the comick kind to defend." He warns the reader in elaborate mock horror that Walter had these notions at first "upon the footing of mere whims, and of a *vive la Bagatelle*" [1.19.53], but that finally that madman had run them down into perfect systems. Sterne too ran his bagatelle down into a perfect fool's system, but unlike Walter he was a fool of Folly's sort, an artist who controlled his form. If his wry development of the ontological dilemma of Locke's rationalism afforded him, as we have seen, a controlling scheme for dramatic situations, so did Locke's passionate skepticism concerning the pretensions of human reason stimulate his imaginative conception of a fantasy world of chaotic lore in which to display the Shandys. And in considering this desultory, fragmentary, carping satire, the material labeled "trivial" by the collective voice of criticism, we shall have to appreciate the complication of Sterne's apparent adoption of the Scriblerian manner, and particularly the manner of Swift, in his use of trivia.

Stouthearted wonderers at the bland majesty of Swift's intellectual will have so inured themselves to the irony that calls up the final horrors of this world—the King of Luggnagg's grace, for example, to the page who forgot to remove the poison from the floor when a young lord of promise was granted the honor of licking the dust before the royal footstool—that the cry *"vive la Bagatelle"* cannot be appreciated save as just another bitter spasm. But Swift loved trivia—learned junk, chambermaids' prattle and all vulgar idioms, the formless shows of things— perhaps because trivia suggested to him a guilelessly insane world useful to juxtapose to the guileful insanity of perverted reason and will which he saw around him. Sterne's stock of urbanity, his moral assurance, was certainly deficient for affecting this grand hauteur of Swift's. Yet large portions of *A Tale of a Tub* and *Tristram Shandy* seem almost interchangeable, so exact is Sterne's feeling for certain aspects of Swift's style and tone.[9] A good portion of *Tristram* is a texture of by-the-way ridicule of learned lumber, of systems, of foolishly innocent poseurs. In Swift's manner (and in the manner of the other Scriblerians) he sets up equivocations, allows us to hear the hum of etceteras from critics, voices of minute philosophers and academicians, indulges in comic and ironic digressions of learned bric-a-brac. But Sterne's bagatelle is finally not a debilitated posturing in Swift's manner. Nor is it merely a cloudy adumbration of Locke's skepticism rhetorically expressed in the *Essay* by constant sneers at "learned rubbish." Sterne loved bagatelle for his own aesthetic reasons, though both Locke and the Augustan satirists stimulated his imagination.

Locke's skepticism, his passion for doubting, shows everywhere in the *Essay* as an emotional rhetoric, not a logic, intended to convince the reader of the need of studying his formula for finding light where our reason fails. The eighteenth century, despite the textbook tag which labels it the Age of Reason, generally shared Locke's skepticism, and especially did the Augustans and their follower, Sterne. His incidental satire is the working of a skeptical mind. Sterne politely despised critics and they have had their revenge upon him with such labels as "trivial," but perhaps this material can be shown more to the credit of Sterne's artistic judgment than can the label to the critics' insight. The Sorbonne doctors, the schoolmen, the law, the Church, the gentry, in short, almost any typical dignity—this is the material good for a passing jibe in any paragraph. How many times does Tristram open a sentence to insert a seemingly irrelevant comment on systems and system builders. One difficulty in appreciating Sterne's bagatelle as a responsible technique is that, unlike Swift, he appears often to go out of his way to mask himself in resolute foolishness, to make all subjects trivial.

It is surprising, for example, how little about Sterne we can learn from his letters because of this very effort to speak in the voice of a character (Yorick, Tristram, a zany, a sentimentalist) and thus avoid a downright statement of anything. He seems to have been sure of himself only when he was being determinedly casual. This device covers well. Except in a few casual remarks, never a mention is there of his creative desires or of his comments on social matters. His background, of course, is precisely of the sort which would make him yearn for the manner of Swift and prevent his obtaining it. A poor relation, beholden to a powerful family, he was inordinately proud of his ancestry and contemptuous of his own station. A lousy prebendary, he called himself. The one thing that comes through the uneasy casualness concerning his creative inspirations is an intense admiration of Swift. There is evidence that he planned originally to travel Tristram through Europe (in the manner of Gulliver, perhaps) in order to make comments on men and manners.[10] He hopes that Tristram Shandy will "swim down the gutter of Time" with the Tale of a Tub [9.8.610]. To Stella he compares Eliza. "Swift has said a hundred things I durst not say—unless I was Dean of St. Patrick's," he writes. One of his special delights in London was recognition by Swift's friend, Lord Bathurst,[11] as the first man of genius fit to follow the great Augustans. The odd prebendary of York Minster, in the mask of the fool, discovered for his own comic vision an odd synthesis of the satiric method of the Scriblerians with Locke's philosophical skepticism. Of course, Sterne's Augustan exemplars, Swift, Pope, Arbuthnot, and Prior, often found their own energy in skeptical thought. Prior, in fact, spares not even Locke. In attacking the schools Locke has only added another confounding system, says Prior.[12] Similarly, Martinus Scriblerus. But Prior's and Arbuthnot's strictures are exceptional, for Locke, who set down the limits of rationalism, was one of the eighteenth century's favorite weapons against learned quacks, and especially against mountebank rationalists of the scholastic stamp. Yet the Augustans are universally concerned with learned bagatelle because they are not finally removed from scholastic habits of mind. Nor is Sterne. Here it is that we discover an aesthetic rationale for his interest in this Augustan manner and in Locke's skepticism. Let us follow parallel (but finally different) devices of Swift and Sterne.

The scholastic habit of finding mystic significances in odd facts gathered by an omnibus learning, the scholastic ability to reason on an unlimited number of sides to any question, Swift turned to his own demonic uses in A Tale of a Tub. His anti-intellectualism is an obvious fact; and that the intellectual habits of scholasticism formed his mind is an equally obvious fact. Allegorical rationalism was in the grain. And fortunately, for since satire is a subversive activity and depends therefore upon the undermining of logical positions, a rationalism which finds symbolic significance on various levels can be turned to the service of a very complex satirical intention. Just as the scholastic mind interpreted phenomena in fourfold significances, so Swift's allegoric satirical method achieves multilevel significances. We may think, for example, of the

passage from *A Tale of a Tub* on the sect of tailor-worshipers (sec. II).
Here within the allegory of Peter, Martin, and Jack is the allegory of a
clothes-religion, and the satirical levels of significance range over religious history, theological tenets, the penchants of human beings for
supporting their extravagances with reason, the superficiality of moral
attitudes (conscience is a pair of breeches, easily slipped down for lewd-
ness or nastiness), human worship of appearance (a bishop is an apt
conjunction of lawn and black satin), etc. Swift's skepticism always
employed the tools of the enemy. Similarly eighteenth-century philosophy reasoned to undermine reason. Locke would banish error by
reasoning away most of the early bases of reason; Berkeley would settle
the "learned dust" by pointing to the reality of reality, perceptions as
perceived, and the impossibility of knowing substance; and Hume
sardonically "manages to chevy Christian mystics and atheists into the
same camp," by undermining the presumptions of both to a common
skepticism.[18] The subversiveness of the eighteenth-century philosophers
is accomplished by rational subversion of reason; often they are quite
as satirical as the satirists.

    Locke, said Sterne, had rid the world of the lumber of a thousand
vulgar errors. "Heat is in proportion to the want of true knowledge,"
Sterne can say, echoing Locke, in moral application to the school-
divinity debates on Slawkenbergius' nose, and at the same time he can
use allegory in Swift's manner. On various allegorical levels the Slawkenbergius epic involves the reader's own assumptions in a satire on
rationalism (can God make two and two five?), on Locke's scheme for
determining ideas, and on anyone's logic ("it proved the stranger's nose
was neither true nor false. This left room for the controversy to go on"),
on pedantry and that scattered and crazy memory of the race which is
scholarship, on religious polemics and practices, on sexual prudery
(and by suggestion there again appears one of the book's fundamental
themes, sterility, the alien worlds of uncoupled minds, bodies, and ages),
and finally, on Walter Shandy's pretension that he is any different from
Toby Shandy, that his rationalism is more than an odd rhetoric by
which he expresses himself (precisely as Toby's military excursions are
his rhetoric). In the tradition of scholasticism the story has various
levels of apprehension. But organically in the whole conception of
*Tristram* the Slawkenbergius story represents by all these allegorical

levels a kind of fantasy world in which one of the principal facts of existence is that we live in a whirl of incoherent and contradictory shards of all the ages' learning. Any stance in such a world is subject to the undermining force of a skeptical sensibility. E. M. Forster[14] has suggested keenly that *Tristram Shandy* is a fantasy in which a fantastic God called Muddle works chaos in ordinary life. Sterne has adapted Swift's technique to call up a chaotic fantasy world in which reason may alienate, confuse, and obfuscate. Slawkenbergius' fable becomes a kind of surrealistic epitome of all the implications of learned jumble in *Tristram*. Sterne calls the reader to an ironic awareness of this darkling plain, and, through his characters, to the way of sympathetic correspondence. It is in such passages as this that Sterne's conceptual use for bagatelle calls both Locke and his Augustan exemplars into service.

But *Tristram Shandy* is a comedy, not a nerve-jangling satire on the human situation, and its incidental satire only makes its doctrine of sympathy artistically necessary. For the Shandys find their way blind in the noon of Enlightenment. (One of the complications of literary history is that the modern term "Enlightenment" is applied to a period which produced so many satirists whose principal study was to denigrate the human reason.) Sterne is in this skeptical tradition, but he also wrote a comedy which is as salutary to the life force as it is deadly to the reason. But the satire is necessary to the comedy, not extrinsic bagatelle. As a rhetorician Sterne had to subvert the reason so that he could persuade his reader of the moral substance of that ultimate sympathy which reconciles the eccentric egos of the Shandy world. Another effort of rhetoric demonstrates that those egos indeed are not eccentric at all, or are at least very similar to that of His Worship the Reader. The undermining skeptical arguments of Hume (which recommend his doctrine of sympathy) find almost a descriptive statement in *Tristram*.

Locke's effort (which Sterne so often reflects) to define the grounds and limits of human knowledge is an expression of an attitude that amounts to a real passion; yet, unlike Sterne's, it is an acerbic passion predicated as a rhetorical proem to his rational solution for man's difficulties in communicating. Sterne, on the other hand, undermined Locke's solution and exploited its absurdities. His sympathy with Locke's skepticism, then, is only *his* rhetorical proem to a solution, very different from Locke's, for man's difficulties in communicating.

The solution is the comedy of the Shandy's real sympathetic correspondence in the midst of their misunderstandings. Thus the incidental
satire in the Augustan manner was made to serve the general comic
scheme built upon a subversion of Locke's philosophy. Adopting the
skeptical attitude of Locke, Sterne pursued it to a total reduction of
Locke's scheme.

In Sterne's peculiar use, the scraps of incidental satire which reflect
both Locke's skepticism and the Augustan manner do suggest a lurking
fantasy world of mad rationalization and private systemization. In this
fantasy world the antics of the Shandys are comedy; in the genteel
decorum of the Enlightenment, they would be only an unrelieved satire
such as the *Memoirs of Scriblerus* or the third book (considered in
isolation) of *Gulliver's Travels*. Sterne's very detachment from the
vortices of eighteenth-century society enabled him to re-create the
ironic but sympathetic world of Erasmus' Folly. To say, then, that the
ubiquitous remarks on systems, on scholars, on churchmen, on gravity,
on scraps of odd philosophies—all the apparent bagatelle—are trivial
and puerile is to say that we need no fantasy in which to see the mad
philosopher Walter, the crazy little military logician Toby and Trim his
mechanical man, the popish medicine-man Slop. The fantasy, of course
is universal, for everywhere men's schemes fail of closure. Such schemes
can be the death of society; for Sterne, this was so only when men
refused to recognize themselves as fools. His rhetoric, like that of
Erasmus, invites the reader to acknowledge himself as fool. Always he
suggests that the Shandys and their world are not wholly eccentric.

Of course the world of learning means to Sterne, as it does to
Rabelais, the drama of man's effort to make sense of things. Things are
more than merely things when they become metaphors and allegories
of the orders that men will make. "What hindrance, hurt, or harm doth
the laudable desire of knowledge bring to any man, were it from a sot,
a pot, a fool, a stool, a winter's mitten, truckle for a pulley, the lid of a
goldsmith's crucible, an oil-bottle, or an old slipper," says Pantagruel,
in urging Panurge to consult a new voice in his long investigation of the
marital problems of individual identity, who is who, how many joys
there are and aren't, and force and faith and cuckoldry.[15] This very
sentence Sterne echoes in defending metaphor and wit,*—and as

---

*See below, chap. iii, p. 70.

Rabelais displays in comic paradoxes all the world's learning on Panurge's problem and thereby reduces to its essential absurdity any manly posture that denies or forgets that women are involved in human nature, satirizes the sixteenth-century hothouse flower of *courtoisie*, but especially shows that men make of learning what they will to dramatize themselves, just so on the subject of Toby's instruction in the right end of a woman by Walter and the reader's instruction by Tristram, or on almost any other subject cluttered with mock-learning in *Tristram Shandy*, Sterne uses learning to suggest both chaos and absurdity and by metaphorical transformation the drama of little men's passions. While the fantasy of total expression, of joyful wish-fulfillment and thirst-quenching by giants is of the essence of Rabelais's learned satire, Sterne, dealing essentially with alienation and comic insufficiency, turns the same material to the representation of interior dramas of small, Cervantic heroes. The fantasy is implied, is the measure of posturing in the probable world. Never does Sterne's use of learned bagatelle merely satirize pedantry. He loved Rabelais and the lesser French *conteurs* such as Bouchet, Bruscambille, De Verville, he rummaged in Burton, because these writers also had larger uses for learned satire.

Yet Sterne is accused of a certain lack of substance for the very reason that he sported with desiccated or nonexistent creeds. "Rabelais," Dr. John Ferriar observed in a prototypical criticism, "derided existing follies; Sterne laughed at exploded opinions."[16] But Sterne no more than Voltaire was attacking philosophy. *Candide* cannot possibly be construed as an assault on Leibniz. It is a mordacious comment on those who fret and fray life for the pleasure of canting, systematical strictures. Desiccated creeds and scraps of recondite knowledge were as good symbols as newly invented faiths for the attitude that Sterne reduced to its essential inanity. All the Shandys (and all the world) swear like madmen. Fortunately they (unlike the world) have a strange perception of their own ineffectualities.

Moreover, since Sterne's sympathy for the animal economy is real, the balance for this indulgence, the prevention of a fatuous mooniness in his own economy, is an elaborate contempt for "the stage-loads of chymical nostrums, and peripatetic lumber, with which, in all ages," quacks have "flattered" the world [5.34.395]. It was simply to his purpose on one level to pick here and there, for in this way he could

ridicule solutions to speculative snarls that are unverifiable in the
Lockean sense and at the same time could erect the fantasy world of
dubious reality which, unlike Locke's philosophy, suggests man's
responsibility to recognize himself as fool. Sterne's Panurgic spirit at
sea in scuds of wind flew at more varieties of attitudinizing than did
Locke, but a skeptical passion animates both. For Sterne, a bishop, a
professional virgin, a critic, a sentimentalist like himself, anyone who
bore a shield blazoned with the straight line of rectitude, in some aspect
everyone, should be ludicrous; like Yorick he had an invincible dislike
for gravity, "a mysterious carriage of the body to cover the defects of
the mind" [1.11.26; cf. *Essay* 4.16.4].

Sterne's ridicule of learning, of academic word-play, and of large
ideas is so parallel to Locke's opinions in the *Essay* that it is instructive
in understanding the original turn of Sterne's skepticism to follow the
philosopher's reasoning. Locke liked to explain to the reader the goads
he felt to set up his system. He announces, rather often, and with
passion, his disdain for scholastic subtleties [3.10.6]. Words, for
Locke, are signs of ideas [3.1.2], and ideas come from experience
[1.1–3]; something founded in substance or in an affection is the
object of the mind in raising ideas [1.1.8; 2.2.3]. But the ultimate
generator of ideas, substance, is the familiar "I-know-not-what." So
the effects of substance, not substance itself, may be known surely in
their simple or compounded manifestations, but we can never know
more than this [2.23]. Thus Locke knows what is the proper object of
knowledge, and what is not. His world is circumscribed. He knows the
place of revelation [4.19.14]: it reinforces reason, and it assures us of
what is "beyond" rational conception, that is, resurrection, heaven, hell,
and the realm of spirits. He knows the place of reason: it can discover
a true moral system [3.11.16–17]. He knows the grounds and limits of
skepticism and the degrees of probability [4.15–16]. And, assured of
God's sun, the steady small glow of his own candle is sufficient to man.

Nevertheless, the use of a candle with aplomb requires efficiency,
and it is for that reason, Locke tells his reader, that he wrote the *Essay*.
In another metaphor: "It is of great use to the sailor to know the length
of his line, though he cannot with it fathom all the depths of the ocean"
[1.1.6]. After he and his friends had come to a stand in their consideration of a subject, they determined that the only way to clear their befud-

dlement was to "examine our own abilities, and see what objects our understandings were or were not fitted to deal with" [Epistle to the Reader]. This, of course, would not solve a problem, but it would prevent charges into the unknowable by philosophical gymnasts. It was a theory of knowledge rather than knowledge itself that Locke sought; his system is critical (and hence useful to a satirist) rather than constructive. Therefore, his purpose: "to inquire into the original, certainty, and extent of human knowledge" [1.1.2]. So did his skepticism take rational form.

Locke is a rationalist at least in the sense that he thinks reason a completely reliable source of a limited knowledge and the only infallible guide for certainty. The restriction on reason is that it has to concern itself with materials given to the mind in a sensory or reflective experience [1]. We can know only our ideas and their relationships to one another. This being the human situation, the spheres in which certainty is possible are indeed very limited [4.3]. Particularly where we most need it, in the world of real entities, both physical and mental, certain knowledge seems impossible. As a consequence, we cannot know *(a)* any necessary relations within things, i.e., how qualities cohere in a thing, or *(b)* necessary relations between things, e.g., the causal relation, if there is such. Perhaps most important, for a consideration of Sterne, we are ignorant of the true inner nature of that immaterial substance which we call mind, and have no way of knowing, indeed, that any mind other than our own exists. Locke's only concession to reality is that despite our lack of ideas we intuitively feel that it exists [4.2.1]. This is a rationalization, a stray thread in his system, and the one most vulnerable on his own principles. But Locke reasons thus concerning the limits of human reason so that he can heap elaborate scorn on those whose reasoning is out of bounds. His philosophy authorizes his contempt for total rationalists.

It is perhaps too much to say that Locke disliked "learned rubbish" so much that he discovered this system to disenfranchise it; but whichever came first, the philosophy or the affection, the two elements are often blended. Certainly this constant spitting at "learned rubbish" which decorates Locke's *Essay* must have been a joyful little drama for Sterne. Though Locke was a sober man, he could hypostatize other men's chimeras as devils in his road. For all his pride in the "historical plain method" and plotted rationalism, and despite his stated intention of ignoring the odd ramblings of the animal spirits, Locke had a passion which exhibits itself everywhere along the history. He wrote for those "not content to live lazily on scraps of begged opinions" [Epistle to the Reader], for those who with him would be content to work as underlaborers "in clearing ground a little, and removing some of the rubbish that lies in the way to knowledge." For knowledge "certainly had been very much more advanced in the world, if the endeavours of ingenious and industrious men had not been much cumbered with the learned but frivolous use of uncouth, affected, or unintelligible terms . . . [which] have so long passed for mysteries of science . . . [and which] with little or no meaning, have, by prescription, such a right to be mistaken for deep learning and height of speculation, that it will not be easy to persuade either those who speak or those who hear them, that they are but the covers of ignorance, and hinderance of true knowledge."

The doctrine of innate ideas (more accurately, principles) which Locke attacks was never held by any respectable philosopher; Locke's elaborate working with it in his famous polemic can only be explained on the basis of his dread of blind prejudice which in the vulgar mind is sometimes dignified as "innate." In other words, here is another aspect of Locke's *rhetorical,* really nonlogical, whatever its pretensions be, polemic against pretenders to knowledge. Sterne as a rhetorician under-stands Locke. "There is scarce anyone . . . ," says Locke, "who hath not some reverenced propositions, which are to him the principles on which he bottoms his reasonings, and by which he judgeth . . . ; which some wanting skill and leisure, and others the inclination, and some being taught that they ought not, to examine, there are few to be found who are not exposed, by their ignorance, laziness, education, or pre-cipitancy, to take them upon trust" [1.3.24]. Akin to his dread of innate principles was the exasperation Locke felt when he considered those who suddenly, without sensation or reflection, found principles planted in them by God [4.19]. Hence he added the analytical chapter on enthusiasm to the fourth edition of the *Essay* because he felt an urge, not entirely philosophical, to say something about those "various ravings."

Since the use of the reason in society depends upon a language that determines ideas precisely (so runs the argument) [3.1.1], Locke became particularly heated when he considered something called "subtlety" in philosophical snarls. Book III, "Of Words," is dotted with flings at the schoolmen, who invented a nomenclature "the apter to produce wonder because it could not be understood." "These learned disputants, these all-knowing doctors" somehow had made their "gibberish prevail with grave and subtle rhetoric." He hawks at any pompous metaphysician with fancy, erudite, recondite names unattached to ideas—"from whence commonly proceeds noise and wrangling . . ." [3.10.22].

The passional life of man Locke considered out of his road. He treats the passions in one short and uneasy chapter [2.20], with an apology that he might have been more discursive. He might, for example, he says, have said something about the "pain from captious, uninstructive wrangling, and the pleasure of rational conversation" [2.20.18]. Such is Locke's passionate dispassion.

Noise and wrangling and rectitude and gravity were a single pannierload of devils to Sterne, which in Lockean cant he proclaimed insupportable, although we know they served him well—served him as form. Obviously it is Sterne's opinion, considered as it is in a hundred passages, that the world is tolerable only when we at last settle down with the fact that the human reason is only a shadowy image of God, is weak and imbecile [8.5.543]. Locke, too, of course, tends in the same direction, but pulls himself up short. A little candle Locke allows us, and then erects such a system that he can say, near the end of the Essay, "Reason must be our last judge and guide in everything" [4.19.14]. On the other hand, nowhere does Sterne suggest any such steady, though small, illumination of chaos. Wherever Locke's skepticism searches out a source of obscurity, Sterne settles, and develops the possibilities of that obscurity into a jibe at system makers or at length into a Toby or Walter. Indeed, he stops not there, but continues, as we have seen, to reduce even Locke's rationalism to confusion. "Professing themselves to be wise, they became fools," is Sterne's text in the profane as well as sacred pulpit. On this text he preaches "The Advantage of Christianity to the World."

There is no one project to which the whole race of mankind is so universally a bubble, as to that of being thought Wise; and the affectation of it is so visible, in men of all complexions, that you every day see some one or other so very solicitous to establish the character, as not to allow himself leisure to do the things which fairly win it;—Expending more art and stratagem to appear so in in the eyes of the world, than what would suffice to make him so in truth.

It is owing to the force of this desire, that you see in general, there is no injury touches a man so sensibly, as an insult upon his parts and capacity: tell a man of other defects, that he wants learning, industry or application,—he will hear your reproof with patience.—Nay you may go further: take him in a proper season, you may tax his morals,—you may tell him he is irregular in his conduct, —passionate or revengeful in his nature,—loose in his principles; deliver it with the gentleness of a friend,—possibly he'll not only bear with you,—but, if ingenuous, he will thank you for your lecture and promise a reformation;—but hint,— hint but at a defect in his intellectuals,—touch but that sore place,—from that moment you are look'd upon as an enemy sent to torment him before his time, and in return may reckon upon his resentment and ill-will for ever . . .[17]

All this is to convince his parishioners that although reason may of itself discover the first cause and a consequent but perhaps imperfect moral system, human passions never suffer it to remain dominant. Consequently, Christianity offers a guide which the well-disposed may, by their will, follow. We need not see this as especially a Lockean derivative or as a dilution of deism: Paul says quite unequivocally that Romans have no excuse for denying God since "the invisible things of him from the creation of the world are clearly seen . . ." [Rom. 1:20]. The point is that Sterne is concerned much less with Christianity, if we are to judge from the space allotted it, than with describing pretenders to wisdom, and less with describing pretenders to wisdom than in making a rhetorical and satiric demonstration of human passions. *Clearly, Sterne's capacity for doubt is his capacity for expression.* Locke was simply a device for amplifying that expression. Locke too is often concerned much less with philosophy than with a rhetorical assault on pretenders to wisdom; but, unlike Locke, Sterne sees a dramatic life-force in the text: "Professing themselves to be wise, they became fools."

What rational account can be rendered of the sudden inflammation of Uncle Toby upon perceiving the Widow? [8.5–6.543 f.]. Tristram runs through old medical lore. But nothing fits. "One would think I took pleasure in running into difficulties of this kind, merely to make fresh experiments of getting out of them." But "the whole is an equivocation; it shews the weakness and imbecility of human reason."

"Reason is half of it sense; and the measure of heaven itself is but

the measure of our present appetites and concoctions" [7.13.494].
Against Locke's dictum that, weak though it be, reason has its proper
activity in the study of morality, this statement displays Sterne's radical-
ism from the Lockean view. However, whenever Locke's formulas fit
the purpose of reinforcing an empirical observation of the passions,
and of deprecating the rational-passional antithesis, they are offered up
as unquestioned assumptions. Walter's eccentric manners in bearing up
under his various vexations need an explanation, says Tristram. Unless
the reader has a great insight into human nature, he will expect standard
reactions from Walter. Explanation? "But mark, madam, we live
amongst riddles and mysteries—the most obvious things, which come
in our way, have dark sides, which the quickest sight cannot penetrate
into; and even the clearest and most exalted understandings amongst
us find ourselves puzzled and at a loss in almost every cranny of nature's
works . . ." [4.17.293]. At this point Walter's mind is inscrutable,
though we learn in a volume or two to read it. And we learn, without a
single determinate idea, from a context of situations.

And this sort of skepticism is a refrain that is sung whenever a
learned disputant is to be considered. "It is the nature of an hypothesis,"
says Tristram, ". . . that it assimilates everything to itself as proper
nourishment; . . . it generally grows the stronger by everything you
see, hear, read, or understand. This is of great use." [2.19.151.] It
unriddles the observations of "monstrous heads,—shewing *a priori,* it
could not be otherwise." Schoolmen and Walter, for example, know all
about noses—including their allegorical significance. Does a nose have
a soul, can it think? Can matter think? [4.Slawkenbergius' Tale.263].

The remedy, Locke conceives, for our blind gropings after knowledge is a sedulous application of the principles of judgment. Here is the
empirical side of his philosophy, concerned with probabilities. "Probability is the appearance of agreement [of ideas] upon fallible proofs"
[4.15.1]. The proofs being not constant and immutable, or at least not
perceived to be so, predications from them must be based upon a
diligent examination of all probable agreements or disagreements
among ideas. This technical use of judgment, Locke opposes to wit,
which is a mere recognition of superficial congruence among ideas,
without exhaustive analysis. Obviously, then, wit is no guide in "this
twilight state" of life.

But when "the judgment is surprised by the imagination," Tristram says, "I defy the best cabbage planter that ever existed . . . to go on coolly, critically, and canonically, planting his cabbages one by one, in straight lines, and stoical distances, especially if slits in petticoats are unsew'd up . . . " [8.1.539]. So was Phutatorius' judgment subverted upon his reception of the hot chestnut.* In such overwhelmings of the judgment, wit may tell us something of the phenomenal chaos. As wit for Sterne is a description of experience in terms of unlikely relations, Locke's judgment is not exclusively the light in the probable world.

---

*See below, chap. ii, p. 49; chap. vi, pp. 109 ff.

# CHAPTER TWO • *Sterne's Use of Locke in Character and Situation*

## 1. Some General Conclusions

LOCKE's omission, or excision, of the passional life is calculated. He views the passions as aberrations, formidable but vulnerable. This severity is logical since he considers it unquestionable that one's reason should analyze the passions in terms of simple ideas involved, and there's an end on the passions. This does not mean that Locke is solely committed to "Old Midnight's Sister, Contemplation Sage, (Queen of the rugged brow and stern-fixed eye)," but it does mean, says an uncritical follower of the philosopher, that "our intellectual or rational *Powers* need some Assistance . . . because they are so frail and fallible in the present State; . . . we are deceived by our Senses, by our Imaginations, by our Passions and Appetites . . . " This particular offer of Assistance is Watts's *Logick: or, The Right Use of Reason,*[1] a system, despite its use of the paraphernalia received from traditional logic, rigidly formed by the Lockean matrix. This ordinary, almost vulgar, adaptation of Locke's attitude and method seems to have remained perfectly respectable during the next half century; for another prominent logic, Duncan's,[2] appearing

as late as 1776, is almost a paraphrase of the *Essay*. So astringent a
view of right reason in its dominion, established by divine law, over the
animal economy was, of course, suggestive of comedy not to Sterne
alone. Mrs. Waters, for example, newly emboldened by a little touch
of Tom Jones in the night, screams, as Tom sallies from her bed against
an intruder, " 'Murder!' 'Robbery!' and more frequently 'Rape!',
which last some, perhaps, may wonder she should mention, who do
not consider that these words of exclamation are used by ladies in a
fright, as fa, la, la, ra, da, etc., are in music, only as the vehicles of
sound, *and without any fixed ideas* . . . "[3] And Square and Thwackum
do a dance on jargon, as the former insists upon a philosopher's right
to more than "vague and uncertain signification."[4]

Still, Fielding's several references to Locke indicate no more than
that he esteemed the man as the very idea of rational sobriety. Mrs.
Waters, Square, and Thwackum are merely ludicrous aberrations. But
in Sterne's conceptual transmutation of Locke, characters are not fools
to Everyman's good sense; they are, by reason of their fatal humanity,
Everyman as fool. Their difficulties with Locke arise from a genetic
weakness. The race is fallible. If we think of passion as a settling into
one's own nature, such absolute control of the passions by a rational
system as Locke proposes becomes unnatural or, at the least, impossible. Of course, Locke was not so un-sane as to insist upon the
operation of his system in every activity of life; but Sterne's hyperbolic
application to every activity of life from generation to death is at once
the sign of his own conception and the broad flout necessary to comedy.
Indeed, it is possible to speak of the *Essay* as the formal cause of
*Tristram* just because Sterne had no debilitating qualms about his
extravagant pursuit of the *Essay's* ultimate logic. The possible difficulties in Locke's rational code as Sterne develops them become Walter,
Toby, Trim, and Mrs. Shandy, although the Shandys, of course, are
more than merely personified baffles of the *Essay's* method. They are
sympathetic characters, for instance, and sympathy arises from the
appreciation of the behavior patterns of common humanity. Because
his figures are sympathetic from any point of view, Sterne must have
succeeded in making probable the wildly extravagant Shandy passions.

Curiously, he has accomplished this by taking those situations
which on Locke's terms would lead to total noncommunication, and

shown them as attempts at personal expression which are communicable not as words but as situations. For example, while it is impossible for Toby to explain (although he attempts an explanation) [6.32.459] the personal logic of his military symbolism, he can impress upon Walter the predictability of his total behavior pattern. Toby does not lurk, skulk, or hover. He is not ambivalent, covert, or apologetic. And his associating passion is one which, Locke himself tells us [2.33.4], is the experience of all men in the ordinary affairs of life. For Locke this is a regrettable *but* natural danger to rationality, for Sterne a necessary *and* natural mode of self-expression: "My dear uncle Toby . . . Thou . . . devoured'st no man's bread: gently . . . did'st thou amble round the little circle of thy pleasures . . . ";—*"De gustibus non est disputandum;*—that is, there is no disputing against HOBBY-HORSES" [3.34.224; 1.8.13]. Like all satirists, Sterne creates a world of *places*, in which a man is no more (and no less) than the station into which he settles by reason of his nature.

Just so with all the Lockean springs of irrationality does Sterne exhibit probable, ingenuous, and characteristic passions. There is a certain complication in this attitude: if we look for yes-and-no morality, Sterne is likely to appear just muddled. Toby, for example again, is *not* a model for Everyman; he is a model for a man with his own talents placed in his own situation. Given Locke's system, considering it, Sterne saw it as the other side of his shield. Does not Locke attempt to show men the little they can hold certain or probable? Does not Sterne pick up the unsure, unsafe, unsteady part of experience (according to Locke) and show what men make of it? As severely as Locke limits the reason, he yet finds that "little candle" sufficient for our purposes while we train for our future angelic stations. We blunder sadly, though not necessarily, because we put out the candle. But in Locke's "twilight of obscurity," like all well-trained comic figures, the Shandeans—each occupied in being very fallible according to his peculiar genius—find their places. There are no tragically blind or romantically free spirits in this comic world; there are only extravagant humorists who find out each other and themselves.

This is the way that Sterne followed Locke and yet made life whole. A man, for Sterne, must be ridiculous and yet be a man, with the small, the real, dignity of man. Sterne had an Erasmian double vision, which while in no way corrupting individual integrity yet insists that one praise himself as a fool. The province of experience which Sterne took for his subject is that implied when Locke, as a logical conclusion of his philosophy, writes that "the right use of judgment is mutual charity and forbearance in a necessary diversity of opinion." "We should do well to commiserate our mutual ignorance, and endeavour to remove it in all the gentle and fair ways of information . . . For where is the man that has uncontestable evidence of the truth of all that he holds, or of the falsehood of all he condemns; or can say, that he has examined to the bottom all his own or other men's opinions?" [4.16.4.]

## 2.  The Origin of Ideas

This province of experience, the Shandys' "disastrous world," we can best enter by following the logic of Locke's *Essay,* noting Sterne's development from it.

Locke begins at the beginning: "I shall imagine I have not wholly misemployed myself . . . if, in this historical, plain method, I can give any account of the ways whereby our understandings come to attain those notions of things we have . . . " [1.1.2].

But there is a digression, usurping some fifty pages of small type, all of Book I, to be accomplished before Locke can settle to his announced task. This disturbance is the famous polemic against innate ideas and against "some men" who hold the doctrine of connate notions "stamped upon the mind" [1.2.1]. Since obviously it is impossible to write a plain history of innate ideas, the possessor being the sole and final authority for their description, the admission of this doctrine would be fatal to any normative view of human psychology. That is clear enough until we wonder just what "innate principles" are and who "some men" are. The view Locke attacks is, in truth, an argument against vulgar philosophies, which may give patent to hypocrisy and delusion. Again Locke's passion for exposing trumpery is involved.

Such a polemical flight might well have done Sterne for satire on enthusiasts or mystics, but since such univocal satire uses a yes-or-no morality it denies sympathy and the ironic overtones of dubious reality; and an ironic sympathy is Sterne's distinct achievement. By definition innate ideas involve mystery, and secret preserves and motives, the very

antithesis of the open organizations of the Shandys. Inspired enthusiasts, holy or profane, were a matter different from irrational humorists
—anathema to both Sterne and Locke.[5] But from this consonance
Sterne takes his own way; for in the Shandean rationale the philosophy
of innate ideas serves only (in a direct parody of Locke) to set off the
elementary nature of Toby, who, "of all men in the world, troubled his
brain the least with abstruse thinking; . . . how we came by . . .
ideas,—or of what stuff they were made,—or whether they were born
with us,—or we pick'd them up afterwards as we went along,—or
whether we did it in frocks,—or not till we had got into breeches . . .
Desperate and unconquerable [Locke's terminology] theories [upon
which] so many fine heads have been turned and crack'd,—never did
my uncle Toby's the least injury at all; my father knew it,—and was no
less surprised, than he was disappointed with my uncle's fortuitous
solution." [3.18.189.]

It was a solution. Something Locke did not consider. "Idiots," says
Locke, "make very few or no propositions, and reason scarce at all."
Outside the military world, Toby's "brain was like damp tinder, and
no spark could possibly take hold"; yet, he is no simple fool, rather, "a
plain man, with nothing but common sense [to] bear up against . . .
science" [*Essay* 2.11.13; *T.S.* 3.39.236, 2.19.154]. He is less likely
than Walter, for example, to tolerate the insinuations of Kysarcii. And
as for science, which Toby alone bears up against, this modern plague
Sterne understood, we have seen, as a real variety of insanity. In his
polemic against innate ideas Locke argues, he considers, the only case
for sanity. This *cordon sanitaire,* really the *sine qua non* of his whole
philosophical system, is not, however, even a real concern for Toby.
Yet this impossible artifact, Toby, becomes by Sterne's dramatic rhetoric a strangely real and sane man, whose desperate humors we see
finally as essentially no different from Walter's, or, indeed, from those
of Madam or His Worship the Reader. Walter's philosophy, we shall
see, is only his rhetorical notice to the world of his ego, as Toby's
emasculated heroics are *his* notice. Thus Sterne claims for the symbolic
urgencies of our egos a role which vitiates Locke's calculated denial of
the place of the passions in the healthy human economy. And, in fact,
the passage just quoted is merely a part of a larger context which uses
Locke's discussion of the origin of ideas as a form for more integral

extended development of character and situation. The context is
Sterne's long working with Locke's notions of time and the association
of ideas.

In some mysterious way, Sterne, who is supposed to have been
unable to think big thoughts like other novelists, was able—so goes the
critical decision—to write a book by borrowing these ideas from Locke.
But though, apparently, these matters *are* Locke to the critics, the
"association of ideas" has nothing essential to do with his philosophy,[6]
nor is it in any sense an epistemology, and Sterne treats his time theory
as a comical thing. Sterne did not *borrow* Locke's ideas; he annihilated
and re-created them. How, then, did Sterne's creation use Locke's
theories on association and time? It is a philosophical use, and its appreciation depends upon the reader's understanding of the implications of
Locke's notions.

After classifying and defining simple ideas as exclusively derived
from sensation and reflection, Locke passes to "made" or complex
ideas [2.12.1]. These are creatures of the active mind. They are
reduced under three heads: modes, substances, and relations. Since all
experience is complex (e.g., one does not experience disembodied
"blue," a simple idea), this realm of "making" ideas is curiously the
realm of real existence. (And as Berkeley was later to develop Locke's
logic, the *only* realm of real existence.)

Every complex idea is a combination of simple ones and is analyz-
able into its elements. This doctrine imposes a terrible burden of proof
on Locke. So he sets about to analyze. One of these analyses, of the
mode of duration or time, Sterne used as a form for his comedy. Modes
are of two sorts, simple and mixed. Simple modes are those composed
of the same simple ideas added together, as an army from soldiers.
Mixed modes are compounded of simple ideas of several kinds, as
beauty. Communication, says Locke, is dependent upon the possible
determinate analysis of every mode. More than a bit of savor is promised in the cracking of the simple mode of duration or time; for, says
Locke, consider the answer of a great man, Augustine, to one who asked
what time was: "Si non rogas intelligo." Augustine, he says, let it go as
a simple, indefinable idea. But Locke will analyze because his epistemology demands: "I doubt not but one of those sources of all our knowledge, viz., sensation and reflection, will be able to furnish us with these

ideas as clear and distinct as many others which are thought much less obscure" [2.14.2].

Then in an analysis of mental operation in regard to our idea of time comes Locke's famous metaphor "a train of ideas": This phrase, a good visual image, of course, caused Sterne to respond. He planted it at intervals from front to back of *Tristram*. Sometimes he draws pictures of a Shandean parade. "In swims Curiosity, beckoning to her damsels to follow—they dive into the centre of the current—Fancy sits musing upon the bank, and with her eyes following the stream, turns straws and bulrushes into masts and bowsprits—And Desire, with vest held up to the knee in one hand, snatches at them, as they swim by her . . . " [8.5.543]. Locke's "train" of course is not a philosophical discovery or premise, but a convenient metaphorical description (ironically convenient for the man who equated metaphor with deceit). Since a good deal of Shandean antics is nonanalyzable mental activity, the metaphor was more properly convenient for Sterne.

Reflection on this train of ideas gives us the idea of succession; and the distance between any two parts of that succession, or between any two ideas in the mind, is duration.

This, fortunately for Sterne, is one of the most unsatisfying of Locke's "determinate" analyses, the main difficulty hinging on Locke's indeterminate use of "idea." Simple ideas presumably are merely passive but determinate perceptions of experience, of sensation or reflection. And men "come to be furnished with fewer or more simple ideas from without, according as the objects they converse with afford greater or less variety; and from the operations of their minds within, according as they more or less reflect on them." The realm of the unconscious is a fabulous place for Locke, and he denies that we have any ideas of which we are not conscious [2.1.1–4; 2.1.7; 1.2.10–12]. As for complex ideas, since they are creatures of the active mind, logically they must appear at different rates as the mind is more or less active. So the assumption from these considerations, that we operate our trains at different speeds, seems warranted. If so, what happens to the measure of time? Nothing very consistent, obviously. A natural conclusion from this confusion is that time is only a function of our mental activity and sensory stimulation, and, Sterne saw, this activity and stimulation can never be determined rationally. Ideas, for Sterne, are an unanalyzable

quickening of mind and passion. For example, having said farewell to cool reason and fair discretion, having given himself up to his ruling passion, Uncle Toby sets out for his bowling green: "Never did lover post down to a belov'd mistress with more heat and expectation" [2.5.98]. This precipitancy occurs right after the surgeon's announcement that his wound would be dried up in five or six weeks. "The sound of as many olympiads twelve hours before, would have convey'd an idea of shorter duration to my uncle Toby's mind" [2.5.93]. Why? Because his mind, with the surgeon's announcement, began to boil with a rapid succession of ideas concerning his plan for getting on with the war at Shandy Hall. Six weeks of martial passion equal forty-eight years of embedded lassitude with scarcely an idea passing by. And this use of Locke suggests an ambiguity in the philosopher's theory: is our time sense merely a function of the mind's conscious activity?

Locke achieves some order in this by assuming that the succession is almost constant in all men; the mind cannot fix long on one invariable idea, nor can it make ideas rush at double pace [2.14.10–13]. (A tantamount denial of his idea of time outlined above.) So Locke seems to say—it is not clear—that psychological time is not variable, since the movement of the train is almost always constant. Of course, this is in contradiction of his earlier discussion of ideas. Certainly, having read this chapter most readers could not but be as baffled as was Augustine without it. That Sterne understood the particular dramatic possibilities in the non-sense of Locke's insistence that the idea of time (like all other ideas) can be analyzed, is obvious when we consider now the context of Tristram's remark, quoted above, that Toby's mind is so curiously regardless of the problem of whether its ideas were furnished innately or with his first breeches or—well, so regardless.

In the drawing room below the theater in which Mrs. Shandy, the good old midwife, and Slop are playing, readying disasters for the incipient Tristram, Walter begins to lecture on duration and its simple modes:

> It is two hours, and ten minutes,—and no more,—cried my father, looking at his watch, since Dr. Slop and Obadiah arrived,—and I know not how it happens, brother Toby,—but to my imagination it seems almost an age. . . .
> Though my father said, "he knew not how it happen'd,"—yet he knew very well, how it happen'd;—and at the instant he spoke it, was pre-determined in his mind, to give my uncle Toby a clear account of the matter by a metaphysical

dissertation upon the subject of duration and its simple modes. . . . "I know not how it happens,—cried my father,—but it seems an age."

Then comes the blow:

—'Tis owing, entirely, quoth my uncle Toby, to the succession of our ideas. [3.18.188–189]

Walter reasoned upon everything, and this hypothesis was one of his exquisitely joyful possessions. He "had not the least apprehension of having it snatched out of his hands by my uncle Toby." For Toby never troubled his brains, says Tristram, with "desperate and inconsequential theories" on the origin of ideas. Walter, his sweet plum now shriveled and bitter, asks,

Do you understand the theory of that affair? . . .
Not I, quoth my uncle . . .
—But you have some ideas, said my father, of what you talk about?—
No more than my horse, replied my uncle Toby.

Obviously Toby has learned the routine. It is a situation—stimulus, response. It is canting talk; here is all of Locke's analysis without determining a single idea.

But Walter has a speech and makes it. Unfortunately he mentions "train of ideas." "Train" means artillery to Toby, and Walter's position is hopeless. He throws up Locke's metaphorical explanation of the train of ideas: they "succeed one another in our minds . . . just like the images in the inside of a lanthorn turned round by the heat of a candle" [3.18.191]. Toby, puffing on, sees his ideas as more like a smokejack. Walter stops. Where Locke's rationalism is frustrated, Sterne has found a dramatic engine.

Tristram sets the story off with some elaborate irony:

—What a conjuncture was here lost!—My father in one of his best explanatory moods,—in eager pursuit of a metaphysic point into the very regions where clouds and thick darkness would soon have encompassed it about;—my uncle Toby in one of the finest dispositions for it in the world; . . . the ideas . . . all obfuscated and darkened over . . . By the tomb of Lucian . . . my father and my Uncle Toby's discourse upon TIME and ETERNITY,—was a discourse devoutly to be wished for! and the petulancy of my father's humour in putting a stop to it, as he did, was a robbery of the Ontologic treasury, of such a jewel, as no coalition of great occasions and great men, are ever likely to restore to it again. [3.19.191]

The regions of darkness in metaphysics are certainly where Walter was headed with this desperate theory; and it is Locke who leads on—though away from these regions in other moments he has warned wayfarers. Still, all is not lost, for Toby's idea of a smokejack runs strangely in Walter's head and he begins to analyze it and as it goes over and over all his ideas are turned upside down and he falls asleep. And Toby, too, but without analysis, falls asleep, and the brothers, having communicated their ruling passions, are at peace. Sterne's dramatic engine certainly subverts Locke's rationalism; but it does more: it allows the author to present his conflicting characters as vivid personifications of ideas so that those ideas dialectically determine the opinions of Tristram Shandy. The device is so obvious. Here the opposition of Toby and Walter determines the opinion of Tristram Shandy that the "Ontologic treasury" is more graced by the *being* symbolized in personal rhetoric than by the existence of determinate ideas. This dramatic opinion is no sooner realized in the interaction of the personifications of Toby and Walter than, in Sterne's characteristic fashion, the focus shifts, the actors, lately so real, recede into mere stage machinery, and the author comes forward in defense of his witty argument. Is it possible there is any judgment in this book? Wit and judgment "are two operations differing from each other as far as east is from west.—So says Locke,—so are farting and hickuping, say I."

So we see that Locke's ideas of time, suffering a sea change, become merely Sterne's device for a dramatic rhetoric. But Locke's idea is supposed to have something to do with the entire book's time scheme. This matter is of importance to the critics, for they set up *Tristram* as the first novel that explores unconscious psychology, as an anachronistic fiction adumbrating the stream-of-consciousness technique of our time. I suggest that there is nothing unconscious about *Tristram*. The critical issue is simple: either we read *Tristram* as a foolish novel with unaccountable prescience of our most superior modern techniques, or we read it in its eighteenth-century integrity as not a "novel" at all, but rather, a fool's very wise dramatic rhetoric. The issue can be partly explored in the context of another use of Locke's idea of time.

To settle some of the dust we should consider what "time scheme" can mean. It can mean, first, the sequence of events by clock and calendar; that is, Tristram's birth, Walter's departure for his Squiredom,

Toby's battles, Tristram's time of writing, etc. This is an odd affair, but clear with some attention, as Mr. Theodore Baird has demonstrated in a critical article.[7] There is a carefully conceived framework of calendar time throughout the book, and, in fact, Sterne used a particular history of England in planning the scheme. So nothing is out of joint in this sense of time. Secondly, there is Tristram's time sense. This is a mystical thing, as explained by the critics, having something to do with the association of ideas. "What is digression," says one critic, "under the aspect of clock time (the physical life) is progression under the aspect of being time (the associational life) . . . Tristram remembers that he may know."[8] This seems to mean that Tristram calls up events and arranges time according to associational importance in the organization of his personality. So far as the reference is to Locke's theories of association and duration, the whole explanation is perhaps mistaken. In any case, it is difficult to understand what "being time" has to do with Tristram's recounting of events. Consider the birthday. During an hour in the drawing room Uncle Toby is taken through all his activities in the Low Countries. This is a digression to characterize Toby, to establish the reality of his "voice" in Tristram's dialectic.* The very fact that Toby does not change, does not develop, but appears in repetitive situations, different in detail but formally the same, always as a voice in dramatic conflict with other voices, always acting the same role—this very structural fact of *Tristram Shandy* would indicate that Tristram's "being" is not in process of becoming by recollections in tranquillity of Toby or Walter or any Shandy figure. Tristram changes masks frequently enough, but he does not become, he *is,* the facetious rhetor. Since there is no becoming in Tristram's being, he has no "being time." We are in the presence of a reincarnation of Erasmus' Folly (who, incidentally, is also a rhetorician) and not of a Proustian Moi—or of a Joycean hero, either. Tristram can even *be* in three places at once [7.28.515], but he does not thereby call up the Proustian being of purely realized experience objectively re-created by present stimuli. Rather the consciousness of all moments, all occasions, all experiences enables Tristram to *place* any event in a context of dialectically crossed motives. The reader must recognize at once the relativity and yet the integrity of any experience. Thus the long drama of Mrs. Shandy's labor—Tristram's trau-

---

*See below, chaps. vi and vii.

mata, Toby's wars, Walter's opinions—is a drama made possible by the availability in Tristram's ironic consciousness of all occasions of his experience. It is not Tristram's psyche that is in question, but his opinions. Tristram associates not that he may know, but, with a quite conscious and sometimes satanic intention, that the reader may be forced to follow his opinionative argument. This process has nothing to do with Locke's notion of time, except as Tristram uses and subverts Locke's notion as a device for the dramatic alienation of characters and for exhibiting the dubious reality of one moment unrelative to all other moments past and present. Thus Sterne's skeptical development of Locke argues for a contextual theory of communication, a theory in polar opposition to Locke.

The third sense of time seems dependent on the supposition that Locke proposed a psychological time, based on the speed of ideas through the mind. Locke's confusion in this regard has been discussed above, and what Sterne thought about it is discussed now.

I have said that Sterne uses the Lockean phrase "train of ideas" because it is a good metaphor. By itself it has no philosophical or psychological importance. Everyone knows that ideas come and go. But it is reflection on this phenomenon that Locke points to in a philosophical way as explaining our sense of duration.

This sort of hypothesis is of course the veritable essence of the cross on which Walter, in the normal course of things, impales "Truth." For Truth, read Experience. Walter's Lockean exegesis of the mystery of the long drawing-room hours while Tristram is on the way is high comedy. But before considering Sterne it is well to look at a determined critical effort by Mr. Kenneth MacLean[9] to show that the time scheme, in the third sense noted, is based on Locke's theory.

Mr. MacLean's argument is this:

> If November 5, 1718, Tristram's birthday, seems interminably long, it is because the author was conscientiously following a very realistic time scheme, based upon Locke's idea of duration.

Then he quotes the passage from *Tristram* [2.8.103]:

> It is about an hour and a half's tolerable good reading since my uncle Toby rung the bell, when Obadiah was order'd to saddle a horse, and go for Dr. Slop the man-midwife;—so that no one can say, with reason, that I have not allowed Obadiah time enough, poetically speaking, and considering the emergency too,

both to go and come;—tho', morally and truly speaking, the man, perhaps, has scarce had time to get on his boots.

If the hypercritic will go upon this; and is resolved after all to take a pendulum, and measure the true distance betwixt the ringing of the bell, and the rap at the door;—and, after finding it to be no more than two minutes, thirteen seconds, and three fifths,—should take upon him to insult over me for such a breach in the unity, or rather probability, of time;—I would remind him, that the idea of duration and of its simple modes, is got merely from the train and succession of our ideas,—and is the true scholastic pendulum,—and by which, as a scholar, I will be tried in this matter,—abjuring and detesting the jurisdiction of all other pendulums whatever.

Now MacLean:

Before drawing any conclusions from this contradictory statement, it must first be explained that there has not been one and a half hours' tolerable good reading since Obadiah was ordered to go for Dr. Slop. Instead, Sterne has given us just a page or two, a few minutes' reading at the most, which would in no case represent time enough for Obadiah to fetch Dr. Slop, had he not met the man-midwife just outside Shandy-Hall as he was starting for his home eight miles away. His return after two minutes and thirteen and three-fifths seconds tolerable good reading is therefore explicable. If we now examine the time scheme of *Tristram Shandy* in the light of this passage, we shall see that it was Sterne's prodigious intention to make his novel temporally realistic to the minute by providing the reader with one hour's reading for every waking hour in the life of his hero, a program he completed with considerable care and success—through the first day.

Now there are difficulties with this theory even had Mr. MacLean read carefully. But he did not, apparently. It is true that Toby rings the bell a few minutes before the explanation of Tristram's [2.6.99; 1.21.63]. But he *started* to ring it forty pages earlier, when Tristram swerves away on a digression. So it really is an hour and a half's reading time since Toby started to ring the bell—but only two minutes and thirteen and three-fifths seconds real time. We have gone in this hour and a half "from Namur quite across Flanders." Therefore, reading *Tristram* carefully, we are presented with this consequence of Mr. MacLean's theory: it actually took Toby an hour and a half to pull the bell several inches. This is not Captain Shandy, but General Lassitude!

Sterne baits the learned hypercritic by pointing to his lapse from probability (the dramatic unity of time, realistic temporal representation) and then justifies himself for this psychological fantasy by a forced feeding of philosophical pap—"a true scholastic pendulum." Of course the joke is that Locke's theory of duration never suggests that by-the-clock events are to be mixed up with psychological events, that

Obadiahs can be transported eight miles in two minutes by thinking an hour and a half's worth of ideas—whatever that would be. Locke, good, plain soul that he is, would never suggest such farce.

Further, the absurdity is apparent when Sterne, to save himself from being called a fantastical romancer, acquaints the reader that Slop was met at the stable yard instead of eight miles away. So it *was* two minutes and thirteen seconds *by the clock* from the time Toby rang until Slop's appearance, but indeed an hour and a half's reading time. Sterne has encouraged the reader to nod gravely over some Lockean philosophical cant, and then has explained with careful confusion its confusion.

Return now to MacLean:

. . . the first day of Tristram's life ends on page 260, which 260 pages would conceivably take one day to pass as a succession of ideas through the reader's mind.

Aside from the mathematics of the case, the pointless scheme does not correspond to Locke's notion of time, to Sterne's construction of the book, or, most important, to Sterne's conceptual use of the idea of time. Sterne, as ever, kittenish, and in his role of learned satirist, *plays,* uses Locke as his mousetrap, and swallows whole many a learned reader without the slightest rupture of his pedantic skin. This joke, like the Slawkenbergius little mock epic, becomes a fantastic device of Sterne's conceptual rhetoric. The reader must come to realize Shandean time. If you want the unity of time, you cannot have it, says Sterne, in the drama of the intellect. You must be conscious of two time schemes: the clock time for Obadiahs to act their roles, and the timelessness of an ironic conception in which the head-on collision of Obadiah and Slop, with the side incursions of Toby's wars, form a theater of human motives. Using Lockean cant, Sterne confuses His Worship the Reader so that he may know the double reality of time.

But this long, subtle, and ambidextrous passage is merely an example of Sterne's standard method with the reader. "Your Worship" begins an ordinary dry mock, as he encourages us to an assumption, then to reflection upon our own assumption, and finally to a realization of its equivocal nature. We understand in this way that time is not a simple mode as Locke and Walter will have it; and perhaps we realize that the time scheme of the book is that it is without sense of time, since events are an amplification of Tristram's opinions and of his characters, not a revelation of plot, and the characters do not change. The whole is always before us, and since Sterne insists upon the reader's participation in almost every line, we have the perfect irony of a view of the whole, including ourselves.

By the end of the first book Tristram has been conceived, born (although he is later twice born again), installed at Jesus College, and has plotted for him "a set of as pitiful misadventures and cross accidents as ever small HERO sustained"; Yorick's tale is told, including his death on a Cervantic jest (although he appears many times again as part of the Shandy parlor company); Mrs. Shandy is married, impregnated, and set at naught; Toby has already whistled "Lillibullero" and gone off on his Hobby-Horse; Walter has got much typical philosophy and oratory done; and, indeed, the whole parish is on scene and defined as much as it ever will be. Furthermore, the reader has already had scatological questions forced out of him; been advised to come in the room and shut the door; had to admit (being addressed as "My Lord") his own Hobby-Horsical tendencies; been advised to consider the meaning of humility and malice in the case of Poor Yorick; and had to write enough of his own story to fill out a hundred aposiopeses. If we insist upon reckoning time, we travel back and forth, back and forth, over at least fifty years. But obviously, since the reader is presented the whole scene at a time, including a character who is himself, the sense of development, of change, is lost and the sense of dramatic irony is all but complete.

All times are present in conceptual irony. Even the fantasy world of muddled scholastic learning, we have noted, is a part of Sterne's sense of ironic no-time. The scraps of the past ages' erudition juxtaposed alogically annihilate time and progress and development, associate the present with the past, and display universal human motives. Irony must abridge time, since from the ironic view on high the future is not unknown. The title, Your Divinityship, under which the reader acts so often in this book, shows him kin to the Recording Angel who blotted out Toby's naïve violation of the Third Commandment. As such, seeing at once the prospect of everything Shandean, he need not work his mind like a groundling to the solution of mysteries of plot and time. But Sterne's ironic sense of time with its destruction of suspense and plot movement does not produce merely paralyzing paradox,.for in his other character of participant in the mental action of defining motives, attitudes, feelings, and ideas, the reader of course does have some work to do. Sterne's time sense was that of the ironist, not of the psychologist or metaphysician. He saw Locke's determinate idea of time as an *occasion* for his rhetorical drama.

Another easy phrase for the critics of *Tristram* is "association of ideas." A consideration of this matter, like that of time, shows us one more aspect of Sterne's dramatic engine.

At the end of his treatment of ideas, Locke feels admonitory. Having talked of the proper way to put ideas together, how they are assembled by rational men, he warns of a kind of idea madness. This is the famous chapter on the "association of ideas."[10] "Association of ideas" as a phrase is a coinage of Locke's; as an epistemology, a way of learning, it has nothing to do with Locke.

This is important, because in criticisms of Sterne the epistemological use (which is a development of Hume's philosophy) has become confused with Locke's. The structural logic of *Tristram Shandy,* it is said, arises from Tristram's association of ideas as Sterne learned the technique from Locke: Sterne simply wrote as ideas came to him, or made it appear so. But since he insists upon the reader's consideration of the mechanism of each digression, we may depend upon it that they are not, and are not intended to appear to the careful reader, fortuitous, or even casual. The careful reader is one wary of Sterne's rhetorical traps.

By critics who want to say something more intelligible than the standard talk about whimsy, Sterne's method is often vaguely equated to one or another of the "stream-of-consciousness" techniques of our day. All this has to do, of course, with Sterne's vagaries with his subject matter. But the so-called digressions are not discursive renderings of a personal psychical organization; they add up to something very different from merely Tristram's consciousness. I have said that we have the perfect irony of a constant view of the whole, including ourselves. Sterne tries to establish the role of digressions in this technique:

> I was just going, for example, to have given you the great out-lines of my uncle Toby's most whimsical character;—when my aunt Dinah and the coachman came a-cross us, and led us a vagary some millions of miles into the very heart

of the planetary system: Notwithstanding all this you perceive that the drawing of my uncle Toby's character went on gently all the time;—not the great contours of it,—that was impossible,—but some familiar strokes and faint designations of it, were here and there touch'd in, as we went along, so that you are much better acquainted with my uncle Toby now than you was before.

By this contrivance the machinery of my work is of a species by itself; two contrary motions are introduced into it, and reconciled, which were thought to be at variance with each other. In a word, my work is digressive, and it is progressive too,—and at the same time. [1.22.72–73]

His contention is easy to defend. Even the out-of-place chapters are a part of Tristram's elaborate rhetoric that defines the love of Uncle Toby. After all, he has certainly given the reader some idea of his difficulty in getting and transmitting this situation in terms of determinate ideas, as Locke instructs. Two chapters are even blank, to hold the reader at the catastasis awhile so that more rhetorical devices may be employed.

Now these digressions (and there is nothing else in the book) must be brought on by some association of ideas—doubtless they are, since to connect ideas is to associate them,—but it is not Locke's "association of ideas." Digressions were a popular device in the eighteenth century, as Mr. Work shows,[11] and have a long tradition in Renaissance comic works, and these facts, combined with Sterne's pulpit experience, present non-Lockean origins for the vagrant text-and-illustration technique of Tristram. Sterne understood the *galimatias, fatras,* and *coq à l'âne* (terms not synonymous but all including the notion of running nonsense) of Rabelais as a discovery of the way one makes connections in facing the world. Tristram discovers the possibilities for communication largely by associating vagrantly incongruous roles, tales, ideas, emotions. Such activity is of course the very working of the comic imagination. And Sterne's, like Rabelais's, original imagination made of this technique a philosophical comedy. Book III of Rabelais, an object of Sterne's thieving scholarship, is taken up with a series of digressions hinging on Panurge's shifting to the role of a lover debating marriage. He appears in this "prosopopeia" (Rabelais's term) and harries the most unlikely stores of information for his answer: the plot is thin, but the associations create a living world. Stories, images, and words are constantly evolving new conceptions of the theme. At one point in this sequence, associations of ideas are made in an old comic form in which each speaker echoes, with a new meaning, his predecessor's final words. A Colloquy of Erasmus and Beroalde de Verville's *Moyen de parvenir* use this device. It is of course akin to punning, a too common associating trick in *Tristram;* and what other than original development of the "echo" trick are, indeed, the many set-to's between Toby and Walter in which the private associative patterns of each usurp the ideas and words of the other—or the plays on whiskers, nose, and any other subject or term? One of Walter's favorites, Bruscambille's *Pensées facétieuses,* includes a far viler than Shandean ramble through nose associations. So another of Walter's books, Guillaume Bouchet's *Serées* [3.35.225], presents a series of stories making occult thematic associations.[12] Certainly, too, Sterne's interest in Montaigne and Burton must have derived from their maggoty turns and skeptical re-turns, as the mind and imagination directed. Burton simply subsumes all knowledge to a subject, the pertinence of most of which a mortal of ordinary associations would be unlikely to suspect. "Association of ideas," then, was for Sterne an old comedy, not a new-found philosophy; but our interest is in Sterne's unique reformation of antique forms.

We have seen how his comic conception demands the constant ironic juxtaposition of motives, attitudes, and feelings. Now let us reconsider the meaning of Locke's "association of ideas" for Sterne.

Locke is quite clear and quite uncomical on this subject [2.33], clear enough to need no critical "interpretation."

. . . ideas that in themselves are not at all of kin, come to be so united in some men's minds that it is very hard to separate them; they always keep in company, and the one no sooner at any time comes into the understanding, but its associate appears with it; and if there are more than two which are thus united, the whole gang, always inseparable, show themselves together. [2.33.5]

This is a disease:

I shall be pardoned for calling it by so harsh a name as "madness," when it is considered, that opposition to reason deserves that name, and is really madness; and there is scarce a man so free from it but that if he should always, on all occasions, argue or do as in some cases he constantly does, would not be thought fitter for Bedlam than civil conversation. I do not here mean when he is under the power of an unruly passion, but in the steady calm course of his life. [2.33.4]

This is how the madness proceeds:

This strong combination of ideas, not allied by nature, the mind makes in itself either voluntarily or by chance; and hence it comes in different men to be very different, according to their different inclinations, education, interests, etc. Custom settles habits of thinking in the understanding, as well as of determining in the will, and of motions in the body; all which seem to be but trains of motion in the animal spirits, which, once set a-going, continue in the same steps they have been used to, which, by often treading, are worn into a smooth path, and the motion in it becomes easy, and as it were natural. As far as we can comprehend thinking, thus ideas seem to be produced in our minds; or if they are not, this may serve to explain their following one another in an habitual train, when once they are put into that track, as well as it does to explain such motions of the body. [2.33.6]

Some unreasonable passion causes all this, something that prevents rationality. It is irrational, and it is dangerous; it is in no sense a creative activity of the mind. Activity, indeed, is the wrong word, for the phenomenon is passional. Such an association must be built on some powerful impression, graved so deeply in the mind that it forms the course for a monomania.

This is all that Locke ever means by "association of ideas." And although obviously a powerful excitement for Sterne, it is never used structurally—how could it be?—but it is the very being of Toby's characterization. And it is the occasion of scattered jests.

Toby never has a determinate idea; he is never, or almost never, out of the grip of his military associations. Half the frustrations of Walter's life of frustrations arise from slamming into the inexorable stream of Toby's military associations. Thus is Walter cut off in his discourse on time, and thus is the ontologic treasury robbed. Walter has but to let his left hand zigzag to his right pocket for a handkerchief, and Toby is off on the zigzag before Namur. *Toby is exactly Locke's madman.* And yet he is only ludicrous in the way every man *must* be, for he is only creating a situation by which he expresses himself, as every man must. Again, Sterne saw Everyman as fool. He was not convinced that Locke's sober and rational analysis of ideas could provide any ready concourse of minds. Locke would have been shocked. What is the harm, Sterne asks, so long as a man stays on the king's highway with his hobby-horse?

Here again Sterne's fun with Locke does not constitute a dislike or disavowal of the philosopher. As always, he measured Locke by experience and doubted the possibility, or at least the probability, of the rational way. The rational way remains a goal, a desideratum (since it is the basis for ridicule of Aeolists, benign though it is), something like heaven, but the Shandeans live on the earth.

Tristram, too, is a wry consequence of Locke's theory. The lamentable association established by custom, involving Walter, Mrs. Shandy, their marital bed, and the great clock, every reader knows. His consequent ill planting is directly responsible for Tristram's small figure in the world. But still, had he been planted and nurtured with the measured sobriety that Locke recommends in his treatise *On Education,* Sterne suggests in every way that Tristram would have had trials enough. He would then merely have been an analyzing fool instead of a whimsical one.

And yet, though Tristram's associations are never really casual or haphazard, though all have designs on the reader, certainly his narrative achieves the effect of the careless, blithe, and gay raconteur's. His history of the mind is not Locke's history, but it is one informed by the contemporary development of Locke's notion of association-of-ideas madness into an epistemology such as Hume's. Of course, moreover, Sterne's innate sense of metaphor made him know that certain associations reveal normal patterns of thinking, normal because all men have common springs of behavior. Vile as they may be, these associations are not aberrational. Tristram's constant general reflection in the manner of a profane preacher makes this truth evident. The plot, and the subplots, do go forward, but, as Mr. Maynard Mack remarks of Fielding's novels,[13] the plot is imposed in comedy to arrest character and display it. In tragedy, passions must spin the plot, the characters must develop; but in comedy it is the reader's consciousness that matters, "the consciousness of a typicality of all moments, choices, and events. . . . we must not be inside the character but outside him, in a position that compels us to observe discrepancies between the persuasive surfaces of personalities as they see themselves and these personalities as they are. Thus the point of view that ours must be continuous within comedy is not the character's but the author's." Tristram's associations are all; they insinuate themselves into our minds, and we know them for our own. Never whimsical, his associations tell a history of the mind. Walter, Toby, *et al.* are his factors, are symbolic personifications. They make their entrances and exits according to the exigencies of the demonstration at hand. This is the only true meaning that association of ideas has, with respect to Sterne's structure.* Sterne simply saw, as did other contemporaries, that Locke's association-of-ideas madness was also a way to learn. It is Sterne's peculiar artistic conception that sees association as a dialectical drama which defines motives.

Sometimes the burlesque of Locke's determinate ideas seems merely by way of a jest, but as a preacher, we may be sure, Sterne understood the value of a good story to amplify a moral text. Consider the situation of Phutatorius after the famous chestnut had fallen piping hot into the hiatus in his breeches. Ten battalions of animal spirits sent up a continuing volley of ideas as the heat advanced from a genial warmth into the regions of pain. But with all this Lockean intelligence Phutatorius was not able to penetrate the secret reality of the cause of his ideas.

> With the best intelligence which all these messengers could bring him back, Phutatorius was not able to dive into the secret of what was going forwards below, nor could he make any kind of conjecture, what the devil was the matter with it: However, as he knew not what the true cause might turn out, he deemed it most prudent, in the situation he was in at present, to bear it, if possible, like a stoick; . . . —but the sallies of the imagination are ungovernable in things of this kind —a thought instantly darted into his mind, that tho' the anguish had the sensation of glowing heat—it might, notwithstanding that, be a bite as well as a burn; and if so, that possibly a Newt or an Asker, or some such detested reptile, had crept up, and was fastening his teeth—the horrid idea of which, with a fresh glow of pain arising that instant from the chesnut, seized Phutatorius with a sudden panick . . . [4.27.321–322]

What is one to do for the pleasures of a rational, determinate conversation in such a moment? And being a lecher, Phutatorius could think of the event only as a sarcastical stroke of one who would remind him of his pornographic mind. With such a conscience he cannot see the event as an accident and naturally fixes blame on the quite innocent but unfortunately moralistic parson, Yorick, as the planter of the chestnut. Such, for Sterne, is the real history of the mind.

If Phutatorius' guileful and deformed mind arranges experience to its own pleasure, Mrs. Shandy's is quite as disastrous to rational concourse by its imperviousness. Her adamantine nervous system blunts sensation, and, as for reflection, *that* requires activity, which is markedly repugnant to her genius.

---

*This is the demonstration of Part Two of the present work.

It was a consuming vexation to my father, that my mother never asked the meaning of a thing she did not understand.

—That she is not a woman of science, my father would say—is her misfortune—but she might ask a question.—

My mother never did—in short, she went out of the world at last without knowing whether it turned *round*, or stood *still*.

My father had officiously told her above a thousand times which way it was, —but she always forgot. [6.39.472]

The horror of this connubial conversation can be apprehended only with reference to Walter's natural talent as an idea monger. Indeed, though he is everything that disturbs Locke, Walter is himself a resolute, if part-time, Lockean, and in that capacity he turns his talents to the reëndowment of Tristram's brain, the natural genius of which, he fears, was somewhat crushed, if not obliterated, by Mrs. Shandy's pelvis and by Slop's forceps. To restore whatever was pinched out, he conceives for the Tristrapaedia the Northwest Passage to learning, an epistemological engine for stuffing his child's head with ideas [5.42.404]. Logic, says Locke [3.10.7–14], leads not to knowledge, but palliates men's ignorance. So it is with Aristotle's ten predicaments. Yorick presumes, with a smile, that the ten predicaments not accounting sufficiently for the knowledge of geniuses, Walter's engine must be their secret [6.2.409]. Locke notes that the only way to "furnish a child's head with simple ideas, the stuff of thinking, is to expose him to a variety of objects [2.1.6–7]. Locke's Northwest Passage is his theory of language. Walter, seeking to repair Tristram's head, in an illumination after a long dispute with Slop on the subtleties of radical moisture, quotes from Plutarch concerning the wonder of Eudamidas when he heard Xenocrates at seventy-five disputing about wisdom: "If the old man be yet disputing and enquiring about wisdom—what time will he have to make use of it?" Then Walter informs Yorick "that the soul of man has shorter ways of going to work, in furnishing itself with knowledge and instruction, than we generally take with it." The way to stock the minds of children early with ideas is to set them conjugating upon the auxiliary verbs.

Now the use of the *Auxiliaries* is, at once to set the soul a going by herself upon the materials as they are brought her; and by the versability of this great engine, round which they are twisted, to open new tracks of enquiry, and make every idea engender millions. [5.42.407]

Now, by the right use and application of these, continued my father, in which a child's memory should be exercised, there is no one idea can enter his brain how barren soever, but a magazine of conceptions and conclusions may be drawn forth from it. [5.43.406]

. . . Tristram, said he, shall be made to conjugate every word in the dictionary, backwards and forwards the same way;—every word, Yorick, by this means, you see, is converted into a thesis or an hypothesis;—every thesis and hypothesis have an offspring of propositions;—and each proposition has its own consequences and conclusions; every one of which leads the mind on again, into fresh tracks of enquiries and doubtings.—The force of this engine, added my father, is incredible, in opening a child's head. [6.2.409]

Talk about "furnishing" and "stocking" children's minds early with ideas is Lockean cant. Of the origin of determinate ideas in sensation and reflection Sterne manages to say everything that reduces Locke to confusion. Willfulness and sloth can always obscure ideas and prevent precise demonstration, Locke warns. For Sterne, opinion can always rise against Euclid [4.27.322], and the symbolic necessities of the human economy are more compelling than the rational impulse to *determine* exactly everything that can be "known." A man cannot even dress but his ideas get clothed at the same time [9.13.616].

## 3. The Imperfections in Words

With but a touch of petulancy, Locke absolves himself of seeking to separate men from the pleasure of their own guile, obstinacy, and absurdity. "I am not," he declares, "so vain to think that anyone can pretend to attempt the perfect reforming the languages of the world, no, not so much as of his own country, without rendering himself ridiculous" [3.11.2]. (But this caveat in his own behalf did not save Locke from Sterne.) However, even disregarding the wayward nature of men, Locke discovers words to have natural imperfections of their own. Hence was the interruption in his history of the mind known as Book III, "Of Words," forced upon Locke. In this book Locke develops his "simple" theory of language. Having got through a lengthy explanation of the origin of ideas ("Whatever it is which the mind is employed about in thinking") in sense and reflection, and having discussed the "making" from these of complex ideas of modes, substances, and relations, Locke warns here that words are not ideas, but the signs of them. Therefore, if the idea is not clear and determinate, the sign of it can do no more than confound the understanding. A complex idea should be no less clear and determinate than a simple one since we use words to signify not real existence (unknowable) but only our idea of it (knowable). And ideas are always explicable. Gold, Locke would say, is a name we give to a collection of qualities called a nominal essence. This essence, which we can know quite clearly, about which we can with assurance make predications, is opposed to the real. The real essence, being beyond our intellects, we are to give up wrangling about. [3.5–6.]

Walter's hypothesis of noses as mystic and peculiar expressions of human economies leads him far beyond the limits of human knowledge into the lore of the finest scholars [3.37–39.229–237], particularly that of Hafen Slawkenbergius, who reasoned like one of Whitefield's disciples. With Walter's ideas pressing in upon his brain, Toby stands unbowed, being armored by his human frailties,—almost as Locke has announced them: "Whether they were above my Uncle Toby's reason, —or contrary to it,—or that his brain was like wet tinder, and no spark could possibly take hold,—or that it was so full of saps, mines, blinds . . . my father's ideas run on, as much faster than the translation [of Slawkenbergius' Latin], as the translation outmoved my uncle Toby's . . ." [3.39.236–237].

Such "subtility" in science, says Locke, has passed for a virtue, "a virtue indeed which consisting . . . in nothing but the fallacious and illusory use of obscure or deceitful terms, is only fit to make men more conceited in their ignorance and obstinate in their errors" [3.41.5]. And there is no doubt that Sterne was thinking of Locke, for the subsequent chapter of *Tristram Shandy* [3.40] is no more than a long paraphrase of Locke on reasoning; yet Walter is a good man, certainly not a man of deceit and arrogance. All the same, for Locke he would be an illustrative horror. But even worse than this display is Walter's next foray after the delicious spoils of Slawkenbergius. His tale clearly states a true cause of the late most religious altercation between the two universities of Strasburg, Protestant and Popish. It was the stranger's nose —and the reality of its substance. ("Heat is in proportion to the want of true knowledge.")

'Tis above reason, cried the doctors on one side.
'Tis below reason, cried the others.
'Tis faith, cried one.
'Tis a fiddle-stick, said the other.

'Tis possible, cried the one.
'Tis impossible, said the other.
God's power is infinite, cried the Nosarians, he can do anything.
He can do nothing, replied the Antinosarians, which implies contradictions.
He can make matter think . . . He can make two and two five. . . .
'Tis false. . . .
Infinite power is infinite power, said the doctors who maintained the *reality* of the nose. [4.Slawkenbergius' Tale.263–264]

Another imperfection in words muddies our conception of mixed modes: what one signifies may be composed of a great number of variant ideas, so complex as to require real determination if they are to be set down determinately. This assumes, of course, that ideas are static and that their symbolic expression may be defined logically.

But consider the project involved, abandoning rhetoric, in making a reader understand the necessity for Toby's announcement, "I am in love." Now, what *is* the "idea" of "I," or of "love," a very mixed mode, or of the particle "in"? While possibly Locke was never baffled by this problem, Sterne was: it afforded several good chapters of comedy—as all good bafflements usually did for him. Locke determines the passions of love and hatred [2.20.4–5]: "Anyone reflecting upon the thought he has of the delight which any present or absent thing is apt to produce in him, has the idea we call 'love'." "On the contrary," Locke continues, "the thought of the pain which anything present or absent is apt to produce in us, is what we call 'hatred'."

But Uncle Toby had, in the midst of extracting a mote from Mrs. Wadman's venereal eye, a real problem. "Are you to imagine . . . that I shall set out with a description of what love is?" [6.36–37.466–469]. Think it not, says Tristram. And he urges the reader into the "mystick labyrinth" "with the word itself" and "without any other idea of it" than what is common with the world.

Still, the project of compelling appreciation for the relentless softness of the incoming Widow as it overflowed Toby is somewhat more extensive than the room Locke has allowed. It is, in fact, one-fourth of Tristram's tale. Determinate sentences are hard-wrought in such cases. After all, when the Widow first dedicates her appetite to the tasting of Uncle Toby, the Shandean world trembles not a whit less than did the Miltonic when the angels first felt desire. Toby knew he was struck by something more than a definition.

. . . this comes . . . from having half a dozen words for one thing; and so long, as what in this vessel of the human frame, is *Love*—may be *Hatred,* in that —*Sentiment* half a yard higher—and *Nonsense* . . . how can we help ourselves?

Of all moral . . . men . . . who ever soliloquized upon this mystic subject, my uncle Toby was the worst fitted, to have push'd his researches, thro' such a contention of feelings . . . [8.4.542]

In course, but despite Walter's bedeviling lectures on the appetites of the lower parts, on the Platonic loves, and despite Slop's paean to paradisiacal Virginity, even despite Trim's address on liberty (accomplished with the flourish of a stick), Toby marched up abreast of the sofa freighted with the Widow and said, "I am in love." And without a single determinate idea.

At one point Tristram tries Rabelaisian rhetoric to settle the matter [8.13.551]. "Love is—": and then a list of qualifiers, A (for agitating) through R (for ridiculous). "But in short . . . as my father once told my uncle Toby upon the close of a long dissertation upon the subject— 'You can scarce,' said he, 'combine two ideas together upon it, brother Toby, without an hypallage . . .'" [8.13.552].

The compelling nature for Sterne of equivoques is attributed to something called "whimsicality," a design appliquéd on the Sterne-figure by a procession of critics, or to love of sniggering. This must be true, for certainly it is unthinkable that it is the reader who sniggers. Sterne confesses as much a hundred times. Consider the following bit of rhetorical persuasion wherein the author acknowledges his guilt and felicitates the reader upon his purity:

Fortune's mark upon the Shandys, an extravagant affliction, was a nose "shaped, Sir, like an ace of clubs." Tristram's great-grandfather, it will be remembered, by reason of this deficiency, though he had a full inch more nose than *his* father, was obliged to pledge an unconscionable jointure in order to get married. At this point Sterne breaches his tale of the genetic disaster to toy with the reader's imminent suspicions and by the way to satirize Locke's rational system for discovering morality.

Now, before I venture to make use of the word *Nose* a second time,—to avoid all confusion in what will be said upon it, in this interesting part of my story, it may not be amiss to explain my own meaning, and define, with all possible exactness and precision, what I would willingly be understood to mean by the term: being of opinion, that 'tis owing to the negligence and perverseness of writers, in despising this precaution, and to nothing else.—That all the polemical

writings in divinity, are not as clear and demonstrative as those upon a Will o'
the Wisp, or any other sound part of philosophy, and natural pursuit; in order
to which, what have you to do, before you set out, . . . but to give the world a
good definition, and stand to it, of the main word you have most occasion for,—
changing it, Sir, as you would a guinea, into small coin? . . . [or, in Lockean
terminology, "analyzing it, Sir, to its simple ideas"].

In books of strict morality and close reasoning, such as this I am engaged in,
—the neglect is inexcusable; and heaven is my witness, how the world has revenged itself upon me for leaving so many openings to equivocal strictures,—and
for depending so much as I have done, all along, upon the cleanliness of my
reader's imaginations. [3.31.217–218]

Then the definition: "For by the word *Nose,* throughout all this long
chapter of noses, and every other part of my work, where the word
*Nose* occurs,—I declare, by that word I mean a Nose, and nothing
more, or less" [3.31.218].

But—"There are some trains of certain ideas which leave prints of
themselves about our eyes and eye-brows; and there is a consciousness
of it, somewhere about the heart, which serves but to make these etch-
ings the stronger — we see, spell, and put them together without a
dictionary." [5.1.346–347.] That is what happened to whiskers in the
kingdom of Navarre. "The best word, in the best language, of the best
world" may suffer so [5.1.347]. Certainly they *must* suffer "when the
*extreams* of DELICACY, and the *beginnings* of CONCUPISCENCE, hold
their . . . provincial chapter together . . . " [5.1.348].

With *love,* as with *whiskers, nose,* or any other word, one may—
indeed, must—stimulate privy ideas in his respondent. It is clear in
what constant danger determinate communication stands. For Locke,
to define is to set up a sign system for logical exposition. Since signs may
be made exact, Locke sees no reason that language should not be something like mathematics, but for Sterne definition is only possible by
leaving out most of the life of the individual. Though this may be the
desideratum, it is more likely to lead to comedy than communication.
Let, for example, *chastity,* "by nature the gentlest of affections," find
*nose* in its way, and " 'tis like a ramping and roaring lion."

Here is a typical example of Sterne's apparent moral divagation
which so vexes and muddles readers. Faced with this seemingly fuzzy
moral meaning, even the benign reader must sometimes feel that Sterne
is soft. All is bagatelle, says Saintsbury.

Locke's moral stand is never equivocal. Morality, indeed, is as

certainly determined as a mathematical sentence [3.11.16–17], since
it is concerned with modes of simple ideas. Such an idea as "murder" is
a mode, a creature of the mind, with real and nominal essences one and
the same. Therefore, it is absolutely explicable and may be compared
with other modes. On one of his occasions as a Lockean, Walter reduces
Locke to absurdity—explaining murder to Toby.* Sterne, in contrast
to Locke, at one moment satirizes those who confound others, and who
are themselves confounded, by jargon, and at another moment treats
with approbation, or at least indulgence, benighted humor-characters
who have scarcely a determinate idea. Or he may ridicule and approve
simultaneously. At some places the ridicule of Locke's theory of language is more than implicit. We should have more definitions of the
arcane jabber of polemical writings, Tristram says, for then they would
become "as clear as those on a will o' the wisp or any other sound part
of philosophy." And Walter, though he has a seasoning of wisdom, is
made to look farcical as he abuses Trim with straight Lockean cant for
his lack of determinate ideas when the corporal recites the Ten Com-
mandments. Trim, honest, silly soul, simply understood by specific
example [5.32.393]. Abstractions meant nothing to him but particular
cases. Bishop Berkeley could have enlisted Trim as an auxiliary in his
war on Locke's doctrine that determinate ideas of abstractions are
possible.

All this is certainly a precisely conceived criticism of Locke. But it
is mild, pleasant-humored, and unostentatious. For Sterne was easy in
his Lockean orientation. He found comical possibilities in Locke's
theories, and did not for the sake of moral rigidity insist upon a sometimes shifty system. In fact, he seems to have entertained Locke's warn-
ings about loose language only to develop his own conception of humanity. There was danger or absurdity in words without determinate ideas,
but even with determined and resolute definitions communication was
doubtful without going down to the first springs of conduct. Though
Sterne can say with Locke: ". . . 'tis one of the silliest things in
[dissertations], to darken your hypothesis by placing a number of tall,
opake words . . . betwixt your own and your reader's conception"
[3.20.200], yet when Toby proposes to discover his wound, Mrs.
Wadman's rambunctious imagination, signified by blushing, spasms,

---

*See discussion below, p. 61.

speeches, and *sotto voce* resolutions, requires translations dependent
not upon clear definitions, but upon a monstrous rhetorical machinery:
invocations, literary allusions, tales, typographical oddities, philosophy,
and a thousand figures. For "little knowledge" says Tristram, "is got by
mere words" [9.20.624].

Sterne stops up one hole for critics who would wonder publicly how
Toby can be "no fool" at one instant and "such a confused, pudding-
headed, muddle-headed fellow" at the next, by delivering a mock-
Lockean dissertation on confusion of ideas that ends by announcing
that Toby's life was put in jeopardy by words [2.2.87]. Considering
the racket in schools about essence and substance, power and spirit,
about "words of indeterminate sense," the reader is to understand
Toby's perplexities.

The death of Master Bobby and Trim's subsequent oration display
the "junketting piece of work . . . there is, betwixt these [our imagi-
nations] and our seven senses," which work never gets conveyed by
words. "Well might Locke write a chapter upon the imperfections of
words." [*T.S.* 5.7.360; *Essay* 3.9.]

Following that chapter, and another on the abuse of words, Locke
proposes his remedies. They are, as we have already seen, concerned
exclusively with definition: a man shall first have clear ideas annexed to
words before he uses them; he shall apply words in common uses; he
shall, where the mode is complex, declare his ideas by synonymous
terms, by examples of the subject in which the idea inheres, and by
communication of his ideas. (This is for philosophical writing; mer-
chants, lovers, cooks, and tailors may, though confused, make a shift
with vulgar notions.) He shall make ideas of substances "conformable
to things" (by natural history); and he shall use the same word constantly in the same sense. Locke, of course, often does not follow any
of these instructions, save possibly the first, and that the reader cannot
know. What, for example, are the ideas signified by "I" and "existence"?
What is meant by "innate," "in the mind," "essence," "objects beyond
our knowledge," and "ideas conformable to things"? On occasion in
*Tristram,* Sterne observes Locke's uncanonical indulgence in metaphor.

Sterne's precise though elaborate descriptions hang, in large part,
on his wit, his talent for fetching up ("from the coast of Guinea," if
necessary) fantastic metaphors, dangerous instruments to Locke.

Appreciation of Sterne's sport with Walter depends in part upon an understanding of this knack; for Walter, that connoisseur of systems, rhetorician though he is, packs up Locke along with other philosophers. Thus, warming his argument with rhetoric, he projects the famous Northwest Passage to the intellectual world; metaphors are to be rejected in favor of a more fecund method of idea-generation by means of predication with the auxiliary verbs. "The highest stretch of improvement a single word is capable of, is a high metaphor," Walter, the rhetorician, explains to Yorick, "—for which, in my opinion, the idea is generally the worse, and not the better"; Walter the Lockean recovers, "—but be that as it may,—when the mind has done that with it—there is an end,—the mind and the idea are at rest,—until a second idea enters;—and so on." [5.42.405.]

Sterne often had Locke in mind when he started on a description conducted with figures. Working as the historian of the life and opinions of Tristram Shandy, he stops to lament that he cannot melt the critics with Trim's witless sermon on Bobby, which brings to mind Locke's chapter on the imperfection of words. He is about to explain the confusion by a metaphor when he drops it in mock horror, remembering that "there is nothing more dishonest in an historian, than the use of one" [3.23.206–207]. But Sterne-as-Yorick impressed distinct ideas (as Locke recommended) upon his fancy by metaphors (which Locke abhorred) [6.11.428].

This is an epistemology that Locke does not recognize, although he uses it. Some of the most memorable passages of Locke's history of the mind are, in fact, conveyed by metaphor. Sometimes, in fact, Sterne applies his art to the work of heightening Locke's figures, as in the notorious comparison of the faculties of perception to sealing wax in explication of causes of obscurity [*T.S.* 2.2.86; cf. *Essay* 2.29.3], or as in Walter's Lockean lantern simile in explanation of the succession of ideas inside Toby's head [*T.S.* 3.18.191; cf. *Essay* 2.14.9].

Locke's base for his polemical flight against those who made a figure by the arts of disputation [3.10.6–13, 34; 4.7.11] is, of course, his theory of language. What can these skills do but make palatable cheats and confusions in words and set up charlatan professors with a persuasion for their mischievous absurdities? Hear Locke: " . . . if we would speak of things as they are, we must allow that all the art of rhetoric,

besides order and clearness, all the artificial and figurative application
of words eloquence hath invented, are for nothing else but to insinuate
wrong ideas, move the passions, and thereby mislead the judgment . . ."
[3.10.34]. The wit of man so employed may never "want something to
say in opposing or defending any question" [3.10.7]. These are the
precise arguments, of course, by which Aristotle defends rhetoric as the
neutral art.*

While Sterne could be, in his way, as serious as Locke, and for the
same reasons, in desultory slings at such personifications of "learned
ignorance" as Didius the great Church lawyer, Kysarcius the ubiquitous
apologist, and the Roman Catholic casuists of the Sorbonne; nevertheless, while he could share Locke's contempt for learned ignorance, he
nowhere accepts the philosopher's philosophic remedy for the pedantic
ills of the world. Rather, he found an expression for Locke's cavils in a
less astringent manner by creating Walter Shandy; but, far from seeking
a remedy, Sterne was willing and eager to demonstrate that there was
an omnipresent human problem and humane humor in the spectacle of
the wrangler. Walter is, after all, of the genus of Don Quixote and
Panurge. Of course, Walter rides his hobby-horse peaceably and compels no one to get up behind him [1.7.13]. This is Sterne's criterion for
tolerance of absurdity. An unmixed satire appears when imposition and
guile appear. Some of the conspicuous polemical objects of satire are
Didius' great code *De fartandi et illustrandi fallaciis,* Kysarcius' subtle
treatment of the important declensions of baptismal Latin, and the Sorbonne doctors' debate *in utero.* And there are the polemic divines, for
whose characterization Yorick applies Rabelais's story of Gymnast.

But Walter's yeasty culture of hypotheses is not a simple matter.
Walter is wise, he is witty, he is humane—and he is mad. He is mad
because he is cast partly as an exemplification of Locke's criticism of
rhetoric, and yet he is one of nature's decent aberrations. His wit, a gift
of nature, has duped his judgment; he came to take words for things (a
prime Lockean horror) and wall in bagatelle with rhetorical breastworks. For "he was certainly irresistible, both in his orations and dis-
putations;—he was born an orator; . . . Persuasion hung upon his
lips, and the elements of Logick and Rhetorick were so blended up in
him,—and withall, he had so shrewd a guess at the weaknesses and

---

*See below, chap. iv.

passions of his respondent,—that NATURE might have stood up and said—'This man is eloquent!' " [1.19.51–52]. He was, in short, a compendium of all the Lockean terrors. Notice, however, that for Locke a degenerate educational system, which attaches a value to mere disputation, is responsible. But Walter is taught of God. He might have known Cicero, Quintilian, Isocrates, Aristotle, and Longinus, but he didn't. "He knew not so much as in what the difference of an argument *ad ignorantiam,* and an argument *ad hominem* consisted." With Dryden, Sterne was willing to felicitate the English climate for its generation of humorists. Wrangling is in the nature of man, and, indeed, one mode of communicating passions. Where Locke would solve humors with reason, Sterne would attempt nothing more than description. Every man, Sterne would show, must create his own rhetoric.

Though "his rhetoric and conduct were at perpetual handy-cuffs," Walter spent most of his time in the rhetorical field. There were a thousand notions to defend against no one. In such a circumstance, for his defenses "he would fly to whatever he could lay his hands on,—and in a word, would intrench himself and fortify them round with as many circumvallations and breastworks, as my uncle Toby would a citadel." Similarly, in his way, Locke: "there is no such way to gain admittance, or give defence to strange and absurd doctrines, as to guard them round about with legions of obscure, doubtful, and undefined words; which yet make these retreats more like the dens of robbers, or holes of foxes, than the fortresses of fair warriors" [3.10.9].

Against this, Sterne's independent use of Locke has created the rhetorician, as a humorist, and sometimes a wise one with real insights, and not simply as a fox.

My father was as proud of his eloquence as Marcus Tullius Cicero could be for his life, and for aught I am convinced of to the contrary at present, with as much reason: it was indeed his strength—and his weakness too. His strength—for he was by nature eloquent,—and his weakness—for he was hourly a dupe to it; and provided an occasion in life would but permit him to shew his talents, or say either a wise thing, a witty, or a shrewd one . . . he had all he wanted.—A blessing which tied up my father's tongue, and a misfortune which set it loose with a good grace, were pretty equal: sometimes, indeed, the misfortune was the better of the two; for instance, where the pleasure of the harangue was as *ten,* and the pain of the misfortune but as *five*—my father gained half in half, and consequently was as well again off, as it never had befallen him. [5.3.352]

For his bastard philosophy Walter carries the shibboleth *Amicus*

*Plato sed magis amica veritas.* This leads him to hale Toby *in Foro Scientiae* for his failure to understand the word "death" in its relations. Toby is inclined to feel that sacrifice of a life for a hypothesis, an idea not uncongenial in theory to Walter, is downright murder. Calling up Locke, surely, to remind himself that murder is a relational word, Walter corrects his brother by pointing out that such a sacrifice, since in the scientific rather than social relation, is only Death [1.21.69]. But Toby has his peculiar rhetoric to answer. "And since the end of disputation is more to silence than convince," and Toby's is one of the best unanswerable arguments, Tristram throws it into the logical treasury. Toby's rhetoric consists of the *Argumentum Fistulatorum.* The tune is, of course, "Lillibullero." This new principle of logic accomplishes all that Locke believes is accomplished in the scholastic system of logical argumentation by the force of maxims: "they are of very little use for enlightening the understanding [but] it is true . . . they sometimes serve in argumentation to stop a wrangler's mouth, by showing the absurdity of what he saith . . ." [4.7.11].

In the close session between Trim and Toby on marriage and liberty, it is Trim who, flourishing his stick, strikes a greater blow for freedom than could a thousand of Walter's subtle syllogisms. At Bobby's bier, too, Trim's artless clap on the heart with mere gesture is contrasted with Walter's rhetorical harangue. *Both* are impressive. Walter gets enmeshed in the pleasurable toils of his rhetoric, and Trim perfectly moves and confuses the kitchen family. Walter's rhetoric is, precisely as is Trim's gestical eloquence, an emotional experience and communicable, though nondeterminate, expression. This is the essence of Sterne's conception of the humor character. The parallel, then, between Trim the sentimental noodle and Walter the rhetorical gymnast is that both live by the symbolic expression of their passions, in Sterne's language, by their hobby-horses, an ironical situation, surely, in the case of the philosopher and a more simply humorous one in the case of the biddable corporal. Neither has any determinate ideas, but each has his peculiar hold on truth. In ironic correspondence to Locke's stricture, Sterne has shown the possibilities of nonsense—or nonmeaning—in formal logic. He has shown the possibilities of communication.

# CHAPTER THREE • *Wit and Sentimentalism in the Shandean World*

STERNE'S rather complicated use of Locke gave form, certainly, to dramatic situations, but finally, we have seen, these dramatic situations are a part of the rhetorical dialectic by which we understand his opinions. To read the book merely for its great originals of character is simply to ignore all the dialectical play which forms the context for those characters. The preacher is in the pulpit, profane though it be, all the while. For although Sterne did not pass off principles as literature, and although his book is indeed uncanonical, there is yet something very suggestive of the byroad curate in it.

As a teacher of mundane morality in *Tristram Shandy* Sterne was not interested in arguing for new systems or even for the old ones. His opinions seem to be concerned on the one hand with sapping the fast preserves of minds shut up from any intelligence of their own structure, and on the other with establishing a conceptual world in which idiosyncratic minds can be related by universal principles. For the instrument to this purpose he chose a rhetorical wit which could discover the deceptions of language. Where Locke tries to remove the ambiguities of communication, Sterne merely tries to make the reader aware of them by posing a human situation and developing from it the tangled attitudes that might be imagined by a mind with a supreme talent for subtilizing. Exhibited in their social tangles, then, what otherwise would seem to be private and devious affections can be seen as universal principles for a history of the mind. And morality depends upon universals. For example:

*Text:* "The extreams of Delicacy, and the beginnings of Concupiscence" are usually one affection. *Confirmation:* The chapter upon Whiskers—wherein is made a clear demonstration of how "the best word, in the best language of the best world" may become "absolutely unfit for use." [5.1.347.]

*Text:* Total inconsistencies in a man's character are usually reducible as natural consequences of his ruling passion. *Confirmation:* The story of Walter Shandy's valedictory, upon the death of his eldest son, Bobbie, showing how rhetoric may overthrow the greatest sorrow. [5.3.352 ff.]

*Text:* "When to gratify a private appetite, it is once resolved upon, that an innocent and an helpless creature shall be sacrificed, 'tis an easy matter to pick up sticks enough from any thicket where it has strayed, to make a fire to offer it up with." *Confirmation:* The story of Yorick's catastrophe, showing the inevitable result of open war on Gravity, the protector of Ignorance. [1.12.27–32.]

All this is certainly to the end of persuasion, and the method is all the arts of rhetoric employed soberly and facetiously, for their worth and their worthlessness. When we consider that Locke believed all morality to be discoverable by the rational analysis of ideas and therefore explicable in a language of absolutely determinate significations, a remarkable epistemological disjunction between Sterne and Locke is apparent. Locke naturally found execrable anything suggestive of art in serious persuasion. His lamentation in this regard is extremely doleful. "It is vain," he sighs, "to find fault with those arts of deceiving wherein men find pleasure to be deceived." Thereupon, as we have seen, he proceeds immediately, in the face of vanity, to Book III, "Of Words," which is a bookful of faultfinding. Nevertheless, Sterne wanted to instruct,[1] using what Locke calls "the art of deceiving." Perhaps he did believe that Locke's system was the better way for completely rational men, but as a curate of souls he apparently saw very few Houyhnhyms, and for this reason defended his rhetorical wit as a way of teaching. No more than Swift was Sterne content to rest in Utopia. In a letter to a friend he spoke of his theory of the efficacy of a witty "theologic flap upon the heart," added that a flap of that sort is not necessary where a man has the wit to be honest, and remarked, "This makes for my hypothesis of wit and judgment."[2] Since *Tristram* is nothing if not a series of witty profane flaps upon the heart, it is not difficult to see why he there takes such lengthy issue with Locke on the matter of wit and judgment. His didactic inclination is understandable, for, after all, he was ordained by Divine sanction to the teaching profession, and there is no evidence that he failed his duty. And Tristram's opinions find expression in a rhetoric not really different from that of Sterne's sermons, sermons which without exception are guides for the society of men. His dramatic rhetoric, in short, was *conceived* to instruct.* Thomas Gray noted wisely that in the sermons "you see him often tottering on the verge of laughter, and ready to throw his periwig in the face of his audience."[3] Now, although there is no impiety, there are no jests in Sterne's sermons, yet Gray's comment is one of real discernment. For everywhere in his sermons, through the devices of rhetoric Sterne leads his audience into an attitude or affection which he immediately turns against it by a change in tone, by irony, by making light of the devices just used. In general, he makes his audience accept something dubious in any proposition under inspection. This method at times can be quite daring. "It is better to go to the house of mourning, than to the house of feasting," says the author of *Ecclesiastes*. "That I deny," says Sterne in the commencement of his commentary.[4] Then he is off on a whirl through a dozen complications lurking in the Scriptural injunction. This is his way of persuasion; it is essentially the language of ridicule, and in *Tristram Shandy* Sterne found the proper medium. This was his genius and he admired it. In fact, so enamored was he of his own wit that on dozens of pages in *Tristram* he takes time out to remind the reader of the clever rhetorical figure just accomplished. At the start of an equivocation of precious nicety on the meaning of an aposiopesis, he asks the reader to consider the possible delicacy of this figure: "Just heaven! how does the *Poco più* and the *Poco meno* of the Italian

---

*See below, chap. v.

artists; the insensible MORE or LESS, determine the precise line of beauty in the sentence, as well as in the statue! . . . O my countrymen!—be nice;—be cautious of your language;—and never, O! never let it be forgotten upon what small particles your eloquence and your fame depend" [2.6.100]. With such a conception of the crooked ways of persuasion among men, Sterne was bound to be hard pressed to reconcile his other admiration, the philosopher whose glory it was "to free the world from the lumber of a thousand vulgar errors," and whose whole study was to remove ambiguity from communication among men [3.20.202].

Since his own homiletic style, which he obviously considered effective, was utterly at odds with Locke's theories, Sterne's long dispute in Volume III [3.20.192 ff.] with the philosopher over the didactic uses for wit is not, we have said, difficult to understand. For Locke had denied to rhetorical wit any didactic rights; "denied" indeed is understatement, for in his own words the judgment runs thus: ". . . all the artificial and figurative application of words eloquence hath invented are for nothing else but to insinuate wrong ideas . . . and so indeed are perfect cheats . . ." Then, as he warns, Locke (with unconscious irony) lets the matter go with a polemic punctuated by a final figurative application:

. . . the books of rhetoric which abound in the world will instruct . . . how little the preservation and improvement of truth and knowledge is the care and concern of mankind. . . . It is evident how much men love to deceive and be deceived, since rhetoric, that powerful instrument of error and deceit, has its established professors, is publicly taught, and has always been had in great reputation: and I doubt not but it will be thought great boldness, if not brutality, in me to have said thus much against it. Eloquence, like the fair sex, has too prevailing beauties in it to suffer itself ever to be spoken against. [3.10.34]

But Sterne loved his "webs of perplexed words" (Locke's figure for figurative writing), and said so in the course of slightly rebuking himself for the passion:

I know not whether I am entirely free from the fault Ovid is so justly censured for—of being *Nimium ingenii sui amator*. The hint however is right—to sport too much with a man's own wit is surfeiting: like toying with a man's mistress, it may be delightful enough for the inamorato but of little or no entertainment to by-standers. In general I have ever endeavour'd to avoid it, by leaving off as soon as possible whenever a point of humour or wit was started, for fear of saying too much; and tother day a gentleman found fault with me upon that very score

—but yours and my friend Fothergil's judgment upon this head, I hold to be more truly nice and critical—and on that side, it is the safest to err.[5]

The manuscript of this letter shows that Sterne had written first "My friend Fothergil's opinion," but crossed it out for "Judgment," just so conscious was he of Locke's antithesis of wit and judgment.

But in an age when wit was social coin and the standard panoply of nearly every literary adventurer, when its niceties were boldly measured and its shams elaborately decried, we should expect some show of artistic concern over its use from a man who by its use had exported himself from the provinces to metropolitan glory. We may trace Sterne's consciousness of his wit by his workings with the term. In addition to the long quibble with Locke's definition which he carries on in "The Author's Preface," in Volume III, he gives the reader the word "wit" to consider many times.

If a bit waggish, his idea of wit is at least as informative as anything said on the subject during the preceding century. After offering a simile indelicate enough to reduce the traditionally lofty abstractions of wit and judgment to mundane affairs [3.20.193], Sterne admits that he has proved nothing, since the logical code of Didius, the Church lawyer (De fartandi et illustrandi fallaciis), plainly shows that an illustration is no argument.

> . . nor do I maintain the wiping of a looking-glass clean, to be a syllogism; —but you all, may it please your worships, see the better for it,—so that the main good these things [similes] do, is only to clarify the understanding, previous to the application of the argument itself, in order to free it from any little motes, or specks of opacular matter, which if left swimming therein, might hinder a conception and spoil all.

Walter had not read Ramus, but Sterne had; for Ramus, and his followers, who obviously inspired Didius, separated logic from rhetoric, and, of course, "illustrations" (Sterne seems to mean similes) were not admitted to the logical regimen.* But though it be not syllogistic, wit may clear a *conception* of experiences too complex or too imperfectly realized to be relatable by a discursive logic.

But before considering in this light Sterne's specific quarrel with Locke's opinion on wit, let us notice the other uses of this word in *Tristram:* Yorick is satisfied with his slow, loping neo-Rosinante, for

---

*Cf. below, chap. iv.

the slow movement is suitable for drawing up a sermon's arguments: ". . . brisk trotting and slow argumentation, like wit and judgment, [are] two incompatible movements" [1.10.20]. Walter's hypotheses begin in jest but end in earnest; his judgment at length becomes the dupe of his wit [1.19.53]. Did "wit disdain to take a bribe" in the "sacred court" of judgment, conscience might better determine our moral attitudes [2.17.127]. In the "sportive plains" of France, under a genial sun, "the judgment is surprised by the imagination." It may be otherwise in more sober lands [8.1.539].[6]

A tincture of half-irony modifies all these comments: Yorick is no slow logician, nor does he want to be; Walter is not without genius, whatever his wit has done to his judgment; conscience's judgment is overthrown by many passions besides wit; and even in lands and among peoples of a more sober character the judgment may be as imbecile as it is in Provence. As always, Sterne goes in two directions at once; he is half sympathetic, half critical. By the standards of a moral satire, he is guilty of an artistic fault which seems constantly to weaken his work and one which it was the singular glory of his exemplar, Swift, to avoid entirely. But such standards are unfair to Sterne and uninformative in a critical consideration. The equivocal nature of his opinions, I have said, arises from the very essence of his rhetorical genius. There *is* something ambiguous in the terms "wit" and "judgment," and, moreover, the Shandeans are all fractured personalities. They must be, in order to function in the dialectic.*

In other places, the meaning of wit is clear enough: wit is invention, which "befetished" critics cannot understand, since it fits not their rules and compasses [3.12.180]. Walter's wit is all fancy, metaphor, allusion, image, turn, antithesis, and pleasantry [5.6.359]. Wit is the glass for "pedagogues," "governours," "gerund-grinders," and mongers of "husks and shells" of learning to view themselves in their true dimensions [5.32.393]. (This is Shaftesbury's definition in Treatise II of the *Characteristics.*) Wit is something not to be searched for; it comes to genius when it comes [9.12.614].

Clearly, Sterne did not want the reader to forget that he was in the presence of a wit.[7] And, therefore, he must reckon with Locke, who rose to label rhetoric the art of perplexing plain men, and wit rhetoric's

---

*See below, chap. vi.

handmaiden [3.10.34]. (Locke was one of the plain men, children of Ramus, the Royal Society, and Protestant severity, who finally destroyed eighteenth-century wit.)

Sterne's use, in the person of Tristram as well as in that of Walter, Toby, Yorick, and Trim, of rhetorical devices, now soberly and now ludicrously, and his serious, I believe, insistence that he is writing for instruction, certainly explain his elaborate defense, in the face of Locke's authority, of wit's way to the understanding. But the very effort to convince the reader that his wit does not exceed his judgment argues for the importance of Locke in his life and art.

The quality of mind that generates wit is not explained by Locke (since it is of substance, it would be unphilosophical to do so), but the *process* he rejects as dubious, if not dangerous, for seekers after truth. To read his definition and evaluation is to understand why Sterne would make a display of his exception to Locke's strictures:

. . . wit, lying most in the assemblage of ideas, and putting those together with quickness and variety wherein can be found any resemblance or congruity, thereby to make up pleasant pictures and agreeable visions in the fancy; judgment . . . on the other side, in separating carefully one from another ideas wherein can be found the least difference, thereby to avoid being misled by similitude and by affinity to take one thing for another. This is a way of proceeding quite contrary to metaphor and illusion; wherein for the most part lies that entertainment and pleasantry of wit which strikes so lively on the fancy, and therefore [is] so acceptable to all people; because its beauty appears at first sight, and there is required no labour of thought to examine what truth or reason there is in it. The mind, without looking any farther, rests satisfied with the agreeableness of the picture and the gaiety of the fancy: and it is a kind of affront to go about to examine it by the severe rules of truth and good reason; whereby it appears that it consists in something that is not perfectly conformable to them. [2.11.2]

Although it is not clearly distinguished in this passage, "judgment" is a technical term with Locke. Having so severely circumscribed the area of true knowledge through which the reason may push, Locke wistfully concludes that were man to wait on his knowledge he must be most of the time utterly in the dark with "little else to do but sit still and perish" [4.14.1]. Ergo, God has lent us a little twilight: judgment. (Perhaps Sterne noticed here that Locke judges judgment by metaphor, a trick of the fancy which he has previously ruled out of right judgment.) Now the mundane concerns of life, pedestrian affairs, all hinge on judgment rather than knowledge. Though morality, indeed, says Locke, is demonstrable by reason and is therefore knowledge, its application, one presumes, although Locke never settles the question, depends upon judgment. In short, only in church or in his own mind is a man ever out of the world of judgment and in the world of knowledge. Since in his everyday activities one cannot certainly perceive the agreement or disagreement of his ideas (this is knowledge), he must resort to certain fallible "proofs." These are experience (including analogy) and testimony. And Locke gives rules for determining the probability of these "proofs."

Now, for Locke, wit has two obvious differences from judgment. First, wit is a sort of mere start on a careful process of judgment since it perceives the agreement or disagreement of only part of the idea of a complex. Secondly, wit has something to do with quickness; judgment goes forward slowly. Left out of Locke's consideration is the fact that a man of quick parts (wit) may perceive a relation (unsubstantial though it may be) that the man of sober judgment (lumbering in his twilight of reason) may never, even accidentally, bump against. Furthermore, quickness of parts must have some bearing on the efficient accomplishment of so doubtful a process as Locke confesses judgment to be. And, of course, metaphor is often symbolic or conceptual (as Sterne says and shows).

The conclusion that Locke was simply "bubbled" was necessary, obviously. Sterne required for the purposes of his instruction on wit and judgment a choir of anti-Shandeans, and, since it afforded a good year's recruiting, the delay of the Author's Preface until Volume III is perhaps not completely whimsical. "Now, Agelastes," says Tristram, setting up his case, "sayeth, That there may be some wit in it [the book], for aught he knows,—but no judgment at all. . . . How is it possible there should? for wit and judgment in this world never go together." [3.20.193.] Having installed his critics in the respectable Lockean camp, Tristram tells them why they are there. Locke was remiss in his Lockean duty when he came upon the old doctrine of wit and judgment and failed to separate the ideas involved. As a result he added his voice to the cry that wit and judgment are not miscible. The cry, it seems, was raised by "your graver gentry" who, "having little or no choice in aiming at wit," realized they would be naked without judgment. Hence, by "an effort of philosophy," since the witty could not have judgment, "logically" it must reside with the witless.

Since the witty have thus not only been bilked of their judgment, but reviled for their parts, the case for Tristram, who depends upon wit to draw his characters, is insupportable. With Locke's reverend stamp, "this principle has been the Magna Carta of stupidity ever since." But this is not all. Tristram turns his "judgment" to account, and, accepting Locke's night of obscurity, maintains that both wit and judgment are equal luminaries offered by God. This is argument by analogy, says Tristram, since wit and judgment seem to be given to all races according to need. In England, for instance, wit runs as high as the luxuriant humors, and judgment runs as deep as the "whoreson passions" it must govern. This burlesque of the Lockean antithesis between wit and judgment is finished with the *argumentum ex absurdo:*

> My most zealous wish and fervent prayer in your behalf [Anti-Shandeans] . . . is, that the great gifts and endowments both of wit and judgment, with every thing which usually goes along with them,—such as memory, fancy, genius, eloquence, quick parts, and what not, may this precious moment without stint or measure, let or hinderance, be poured down . . . into our brains . . .
> Bless us!—what noble work we should make! . . . But hold . . . I am beginning to foresee . . . that as we shall all of us . . . be great wits . . . there would be so much satire and sarcasm,—scoffing and flouting, . . . and hitting of sore places,—there would be no such thing as living for us.
> But then again, as we should all of us be men of great judgment, we should make up matters as fast as ever they went wrong; and though we should abominate each other . . . we should nevertheless, my dear creatures, be all courtesy and kindness . . . [3.20.194–195]

Alluding to Pantagruel's advice to Panurge to get his information wherever he can find it (from a sot, a pot, a fool, a stool), Tristram picks up a cane chair with two knobs for his illustration. (This is in opposition to Didius' and Ramus' logical code which maintains that an illustration is no argument.)

> —Here stands *wit,*—and there stands *judgment,* close beside it, just like the two knobbs I'm speaking of . . .
> —You see, they are the highest and most ornamental parts of its frame,—as wit and judgment are of ours,—and like them too, indubitably made and fitted to go together . . . *to answer one another.* [3.20.200–201]

Finally there is an appeal to the reader's sense of symmetry in the business of removing first one knob and then the other. Great wigs of judgment may stand alone in their singular knobbiness, but for Shandeans or Rabelaisians there may be a world of significance in a sot, a pot, a fool, a stool. Sterne's defense of *both* wit and judgment as *equal* luminaries offered by God is the *reductio ad absurdum* of a century of argument over the matter.[8] In this book wit makes all the emotion of Yorick's death (he dies on a Cervantick jest); all the urgency of Tristram's sensible apprehension in his journey on the Continent (he makes Death mistake his man by a quick joke); all the satire of Toby's amours (Walter finishes the subject by exposing the impotence of the Town Bull, who, anyone would *think,* might have done for Europa).

His statements in which the term "wit" is used show that he thought of wit as a way for communicating intuitive conceptions as opposed to the discursive determination of logic which is judgment. This idea of wit was often distinguished as "true wit" from "false wit" (puns, quibbles, odd metaphors, pornography, and typographical tricks, used as ends in themselves, *Spectators* 58–63). Hobbes, to whom belongs the distinction of starting the wit-and-judgment antithesis *(Leviathan,* I, 8), yet did not depreciate the work of wit, but insisted that the quality of judgment accompany it, else all is madness. This seems to be approximately Sterne's attitude, but after Hobbes the distinction between wit and judgment came often to be considered (by Locke and others) as a distinction between the irrational and the rational man; hence the antithesis could be used by anyone who wished to belittle the talents of a wit. Or, says Sterne, it came to be the Magna Carta of stupidity, since a man who had no wit could always claim that he had judgment. Such argument is the epistemology of rhetorical wit. The long way Sterne takes to avoid a sober analysis of Locke's "bebubblement" is simply evidence of how well he knew his forte, how carefully he contrived a steady Shandean tone, and, above all, how well he understood the separate uses of logic and rhetoric. Locke, who is himself often (unintentionally) more rhetorical than logical, could find no serious use for rhetorical persuasion.

Sterne's working with the term "wit" is informative for two reasons in relation to his whole conception: He asks that his theory of instruction, through wit—as opposed to Locke's,—should be considered as seriously as any clown's efforts to communicate. And Sterne was convinced of the social necessity of the fool [1.11.24]. Furthermore, he was careful to dispute by specification, not alone by implication, Locke's rational theory of language as the only method of instruction and communication.

That Sterne had a philosophical vision of order for a world of private personalities, and that that order is a moral one, is obvious from his development of the possibilities of Locke's skepticism, from his humor founded on his perception of the inadequacy of Locke's rational solution of the dilemma created by the *Essay's* logic; but obviously with such a critical foundation, if *Tristram Shandy* is concerned with instruction, and with a real order, it must have something positive to offer.[9] It offers to tell us, through contrasts and equivocations, something of our mental life, our irrational associations and conceptions — which matter Locke had not considered; and it offers to tell us there is a possibility, through an understanding of this mental life in its public signs, of sentimental, public communication and understanding among peculiar personalities—which matter Locke had not considered. The characters of the book and the rhetorical play with the reader are in illustration of these meanings.

That Sterne's order is mundane and temporal must be confessed, although if it were not confessed we could use Coleridge, in some comments one of his few really perceptive critics, to support and stiffen Sterne. For Sterne defined the Cervantic humor (which he considered his own) as describing silly and trifling events with the circumstantial pomp of great ones; and commenting on Sterne, Coleridge[10] allowed that this did define the essence of humor—after he had made a slight addition: he merely added infinity, thus: the little is made great, and the great little in order to destroy both—because all is equal in contrast with the infinite. Sterne, who always maintained the double vision of irony, of course did not wish to destroy either the great or the little, and Coleridge was talking about himself when he added infinity.

The mundane limitations of Sterne's cosmos in fact are the very energy of his satire. He was concerned almost exclusively with the problem of communication among men, and found enough fascination in merely exhibiting worldly phenomena for their rare instruction. He sets Uncle Toby skuttering after Galileo and Toricelli, among others, in order to plot the precise road of the cannon ball that did him all the mischief. While the poor noodle is pounding into the mazes, Sterne can come on the scene for his choral apostrophe: " . . . stop! my dear uncle Toby,—stop!—go not one foot further into this thorny and bewilder'd track,— . . . intricate are the troubles which the pursuit of this bewitching phantom, KNOWLEDGE, will bring upon thee.— O my uncle! fly—fly—fly . . ." [2.3.90.] Why fly? and whither? Uncle Toby is sufficient unto himself; he lives in good nature and has a snug world that serves well enough. But if we infer from this tableau that Sterne's conception of the cosmos is one of smugness and solipsism, his "mind" certainly is trivial. He becomes a consumptive, almost consumed, butterfly. ("I must . . . attempt to break this butterfly upon the wheel," writes a recent examiner of Sterne.)[11] But Sterne is not ridiculing or complaining about Galileo and Company. Toby is only a particular kind of fool, to be praised but not emulated. Sterne is not proposing the abandonment of rationality. He certainly accepts Locke's definition of the limits of rationalism, but most of life is lived beyond these limits and Locke's advice in these quarters is one thing and Sterne's another.

Sterne's entire ethical conception hinged on his understanding of human motives. This is why much of the activity and description of the book is mental. This is why, too, perhaps, much of it stimulates the reader to thoughts that he can escape only by announcing that his author is obscene. Indeed, it is this understanding and poking up of probable human motives which seems to have led Sterne to the rationale of sentimentalism as a bridge over Locke's separation of one mental substance from another. But "sentimentalism" is today almost certainly a term of abuse, universally understood. Could we not define sentimentalism as Sterne used it and not as a term indicating maudlin self-indulgence? The following definition at least suits Sterne's practice: By sensory apprehension of the behavior of other persons, and by comparing that behavior by an association of ideas with our own, we conceive a sympathy with other persons. Certainly this process is Sterne's whole study in *Tristram Shandy*. And certainly this has nothing to do with self-indulgence, nothing to do with a fatuous, uncritical benevolism, nothing to do with irresponsibility. The limited benevolence (limited to certain creeds) of the later eighteenth-century sentimental comedy cannot be the same thing as this process which admits no particularity or limits. It is perfectly general.[12]

Sterne was not a philosopher, but, curiously, the closest parallel to this view of human concourse is Hume's doctrine of sympathy,—which is not especially surprising, since Hume, too, started with a consideration of the difficulties inherent in Locke's rationalism. We do not know why Hume thought *Tristram Shandy* "the best book that has been writ by any Englishman these thirty years,"[13] but very possibly he saw how near the cleric from the enemy camp had come to his view.

Hume was not an egoist, as was Hobbes, but he believed that all social morals were discoverable and explicable not through reason alone, as Locke maintains, but through a sentimental intuition of customary motives and attitudes. But an imaginative insight through the association of ideas, says Hume, is necessary to achieve this knowledge. As we perceive actions in others similar to our own, we form an idea of the emotions of others, and the idea is transformed into an impression, and becomes through association with ourselves a real passion of our own. But still the emotion or passion is not directed toward ourselves, but rather, we feel for and with the object of our intuition. For Hume man is always a social being, neither egoistic nor selfless but always in some sympathetic relation (in normal behavior). Reason, being not an active faculty, becomes the slave of the passions, in the respect that reason can do nothing without passional intuition.[14]

This philosophical sentimentalism is the real sentimentalism of *Tristram Shandy;* it is the real order of *Tristram Shandy*. When critics find the meaning of the book shallow, invariably they suppose that Sterne is recommending a world of sentimental Tobys. This is taken to be the sentimental lesson of the book. And yet Tristram says twice that not Toby but Walter is preëminently the man of sensibility [2.12.114; 9.1.599]. Furthermore, Toby knows that a gentle Fortune has given him his commission and a hundred and twenty pounds as protection, and that he could not have got along in the world without that favor from Fortune [4.7.277]. Walter and even Trim know that Toby is delusional in his humanity. Nothing contrasts Toby so well to the outside world—and incidentally demonstrates Sterne's attitude—as Walter's observation that "if any mortal in the whole universe had done such a thing [the bowling-green war], except his brother Toby, it would have been looked upon by the world as one of the most refined satyrs upon . . . parade and prancing . . ." [6.22.446]. But the reader, seeing simultaneously the world and Uncle Toby, does look with refined irony. At once he sees the hope in a fool and the despair in the world. Sterne has not argued the moral worth of the doctrine of sympathy; he has proved it, for he has created a group of humor characters with whom *anyone* can have complete sympathy, and *equally important,* whom *no one* would emulate, *least of all Sterne.* The role of Yorick, remember, as it was played about London, was merely part of Sterne's fleering tax on the public.[15] In a sense behind the habit of the fool, Sterne displays in *Tristram Shandy* a thersitical character which could be far more bitter than Swift's in *Gulliver,* because he is less certain of his own premises. What is more bitter than a doubt of nearly every proposition in life? But the integrity of the book is preserved by an objective irony which *respects* every man's personal rhetoric, a Cervantic humor which at once prevents the domination of the thersitical character and preserves from banality the ultimate faith in social sympathy. The core of Sterne's sentimentalism lies in his insistence that by certain public signs—conduct, reaction, and attitude—we can come to understand individuality. Far from any romantic notion of the private personality, this conception is rooted in Aristotle's *Rhetoric* and the whole classical tradition of predictable human behavior. It is to a consideration of Sterne's rhetorical efforts to communicate his ideas that we turn in Part Two.

- *Part Two*

STERNE'S RHETORIC

AS A SYSTEM OF

COMMUNICATION

# CHAPTER FOUR • The Philosophy of Rhetoric

## 1. Rhetoric
## and Belief

THOUGH we discover the formal outlines of the conceptual world of *Tristram Shandy* by understanding Sterne's comic subversion and re-creation of Locke's notions on communication, we realize this world only through the force and vivacity of the impressions which make the texture of the fiction. Part Two of the present work is concerned with this texture, the rhetorical stratagems, the schemes of words and thought, which create belief in the Shandean world. Of course "texture" and "conceptual world" are terms of intellectual distinction and the artistry they describe is a total experience of creative reading. We have already noted, perforce, in discussing the controlling conceptions, the rhetorical patterns of interplay of characters and of the narrator's communication with the reader —those patterns by which Sterne calls us to conscious consideration of the difficulties of personal apprehension. The large rhetorical stratagems, too, of ironic time and association of ideas, which allow constant interplay of voices and occasions, of the skeptical wit which establishes a fantasy world of accident and non-sense where we must, with the author, discover value, are the very definition of this Shandean conceptual world. As a preacher, Sterne knew the crooked ways of persuasion and the possibilities of comedy in rhetorical technique. We have now to consider the uncanonical rhetorical texture of his profane persuasion in *Tristram*.

If, however, *Tristram Shandy* is a rhetorical work, it is so with a difference: the immediate pleasure of the comedy is one difference, but even when we consider the comedy as ultimately part of a large rhetorical persuasion, there is the Shandean oddity that the rhetoric moves through no due course to a conclusion (the book has no beginning, middle, and end). The zany in the pulpit gives us no moral calipers by which to measure this world or the next. (This is not to say, either, that *Tristram* is the work of a nihilistic, though trivial, satanist who persuades us to luxuriate, sensibly, in paralyzing riddles.) When we say that Toby, Walter, Slop, the Widow Wadman, an encyclopedia of learned oddments, a running and vilely probing conversation between ourselves and the narrator—that these elements are realized in one conception,—we pay tribute to Sterne as an artist of wonderful metaphoric and symbolic vision, and not as a preacher. Yet though rhetoric, per se, *is* the art of persuasion and not the art of creating a conceptual world, it is turned to the latter use by the several unorthodox rhetorical processes in *Tristram,* some of them particular effects of other satires, and some peculiar to Sterne's own persuasion.

One of course is that of the *reductio ad absurdum,* an exploration of the lurking enormities in logical stances of all sorts—in *Tristram,* of Locke, of rationalists, of the proprieties of nice people.

By another, we know the characters because they *must* express themselves, each by developing his own persuasion; Walter, indeed, by becoming an abstract of mad rhetoric.

Rhetorical inflation, too, by stylizing, objectifies the sentiments of the narrator and his characters, creating that precious, teetering, ambiguous balance between pathos and bathos which is an important source of Sterne's comedy. In the manner of the mock-heroic, rhetorical inflation can produce the comedy of absurdly disproportionate values which also, slyly, undermine values we think of as nicely proportionate.

The very process of rhetorical dialectic, as the rhetorician proposes question and answer, shifts his ground, communicates with his respondent, leads him to self-implication and exposure—the very process *makes* Socratic irony which can shade from wry realization to paradox to buffoonery. The character of the speaker, one traditional proof of rhetoric, need only become dubious or shifty and real complexities of irony become possible. (In praise of folly, Folly speaks and creates complex conceptions by subtly shifting her ground.) The medley of styles that every rhetorical manual teaches can easily effect with varying emphases persuasion, burlesque, grotesque, or quietly ironic conceptions. (See Pope's *Peri Bathous.*)

In *Tristram,* Sterne, by a texture of rhetorical devices at once serious and comic, synthesizes his conceptual world: Working from the constantly implied topic "How can men express themselves?" the rhetorical dialectic, as it explores the problem in nine books of ironic juxtapositions and fantastic involutions, discovers *relations* among eccentric mental processes. It turns our consciousness not to the end of the argument, but to the process, so that we watch the effects of rhetoric, turn, antithesis, parallel, logic, pathos, inflation, diminution, and so on, as they define characters, motives, attitudes, feelings, in relation to one another and to our own private prejudices and assumptions. Rhetoric becomes the subject of rhetoric, and resolution of the rhetorical logic is not necessary, because we learn by consciousness of the process. The significant continuity of this book is the communication between the reader and his author (through the fool's mask of Tristram), as the author invents his vexed arguments. Always we must know how and why we react to a given stimulus. This is the technique Sterne adapted from his sermons, in which he came to rely on the effect of provoking his parishioners by an argument, usually developed by playing upon standardized reactions, with vivid picturing and personification, and then reminding them of their motives.

In all these senses *Tristram* is rhetorical persuasion which yet, peculiarly, creates a world of conception.

Now Locke's *Essay* was the new logic for the eighteenth century, and logic or reasoning, as a *moral* art, was by Locke as facilely distinguished from rhetoric as was judgment from wit, and this distinction we know Sterne would not accept. "That powerful instrument of error and deceit" [3.10.34], Locke labeled rhetoric, and rigorously forgot the passions in his theory of belief. Sterne developed the forlorn frustra-

tions implicit in Locke's theory, and back into the resultant void
marched the passions—with all rhetorical ostentation. Rhetoric produces a sort of belief, different from that of logic, predicated, as Aristotle
tells us still, not upon necessary propositions, but upon the probable
reactions of men to given propositions. Sterne's comedy asks our consideration of the belief produced by rhetoric, as a symbol, really of our
own mental processes. Thus both the author and the reader must be
self-conscious. Rhetorical proofs are the subject of this drama. But
before we proceed to examine the basic philosophy of rhetorical theory
which bears on the texture of Sterne's comedy, we may find it useful, I
think, to hold in mind a narrow view of two paragraphs of Sterne's
rhetorical play in *Tristram*. In this way, with the ridiculous before us,
we may not overcharge the theory.

## 2. *An Example of "Tristram Shandy's" Rhetoric*

Scarcely is panegyric machinery for poor Yorick mounted [1.11.23]
when, in the middle of an amplification on the conventional rhetorical
topic of the ancient name and honorable establishment of the subject's
family, Tristram interrupts a bit of testimony from "a most antient
account," and, while the sentence hangs, examines it, rejects it, and
tells the reader why. This is a rhetorical stratagem passed down the
centuries as the "epanorthosis" or "correction" by the professors of
the art, acting, as they remind us, upon authority no slighter than
Cicero's and Quintilian's. Still, despite the pedantry requisite even to
say "epanorthosis," it represents a routine universal with small children,
taught, like Walter, of God.

Not all rhetorical figures are so naïve, but all play upon normal
attitudes; and the figures which require the auditor to participate in
the construction of a sentence, of which "correction" is one, are more
than a casual effect in *Tristram Shandy:* a dozen ways and hundreds of
times they ask the reader to consider his normal attitudes. This is one
of the basic forms of Sterne's style. So elementary a rhetoric would be
foolhardy if used solemnly, and only buffoonery if used as pert innu-
endo. But it is not the contention of this discussion that Sterne is either
naïve or exclusively a buffoon.

The panegyric on Yorick is part of a moral story, Tristram tells us,[1]
but this passage is only an insinuation. Antecedent to the discussion of

the man himself, Quintilian instructs, will be amplification on his country, parents, and ancestors,[2] but probability must be the regulative principle of narrative, "for there are many narratives true which are not probable." The inartificial[3] argument from the "antient account," now in perfect preservation, suffers the "correction," then, because Tristram to gain an ethical proof[4] "would not shake [his] credit in telling an improbable truth, however indisputable in itself." (The topics of rhetoric become less important than the psychological fact that rhetoric becomes a topic of rhetoric; the reader becomes his own foil. Sterne thus associates himself with a long tradition of facetious rhetoricians, Erasmus, Rabelais, Cervantes, Shakespeare, Butler, Pope, Fielding.) The argument first appeals to the reader's assumption that a man's ancestry is testimony to his worth; next the probability topic brings the rhetorical process into consciousness with an oblique notice to the reader of the way rhetoric acts upon him, and here begins the process of diminution, diminution of the reader's own assumptions. Tristram continues: Yorick's name has been spelt exactly the same "for I do not know how long; which is more than I would venture to say of one-half of the best surnames in the kingdom." Thus *arriviste* names, one-half of the kingdom's best, are invited to consider their participation in the original rhetorical motive of the proof, that "a man's ancestry testifies to his worth," a proof possibly unsatisfactory to anyone who cannot "stand up and swear, 'that his own great grandfather was the man who did either this or that'." Then a sham enthymeme in the form of a disjunctive rhetorical question, either answer of which is convictive: "Has this [new getting of names] been owing to the pride or to the shame of the proprietors?" Finally, the original motive, aggrandizement by ancestor worship, is completely subverted in the next two paragraphs, in which we are informed that while Yorick family records were intact to show that his ancestor not only was of the same name but held a "considerable post" at court, the "considerable post" was that of jester, so poorly thought of that it has been abolished these two centuries as totally unnecessary. But then, Yorick really is noble and his ancestor's job "considerable" by Shandean values. The reader's underlying assumptions in accepting the panegyric thus stand in view *but not intact*. The argument follows the Sterne pattern: statement and use of implications to examine the grounds of the statement. Always the reader must know that he can be tricked. In the whole panegyric, the figure of Yorick, vaguely crucified, comes to represent, in a complex conception, the value and danger of a jest in a mean world. We are constantly reminded of our own motives. Even Yorick's horse, praised as all heroes' horses must be praised in panegyric, is turned to account: he is a very chaste horse—by reason of his phlegmatic nature. "And let me tell you, Madam, there is a great deal of very good chastity in the world, in behalf of which you could not say more . . . " [1.10.18].

Sterne's rhetorical play upon standardized reactions fell hardest upon the nineteenth century, and its critics have, as a chorus, had their revenge. Always they have referred to sexual matters, but that aspect of Sterne is only a facet of his rhetorical aim, *to discover motives for reactions, by stimulating reactions.* Thackeray nervously objects, "He is always looking in my face, watching his effect . . . ";[5] but Coleridge, though disapproving, was calmer (and keener):

> I would remark that there is a sort of knowingness, the wit of which depends —1st, on the modesty it gives pain to; or 2dly, on the innocence and innocent ignorance over which it triumphs; or, 3dly, *on a certain oscillation in the individual's own mind between the remaining good and the encroaching evil of his nature —a sort of dallying with the devil* . . . so that the mind has in its own white and black angel the same or similar amusement, as may be supposed to take place between an old debauchee and a prude,—she feeling resentment, on the one hand, from a prudential anxiety to preserve appearances and have a character, and, on the other, an inward sympathy with the enemy . . .[6]

Coleridge felt that these satanic tricks were an unfair assault on human nature, transcendentally good as it is, and undoubtedly he was right from his point of view, fundamentally different from Sterne's, as the transcendental is different from the mundane. We can palliate Sterne's crime only by recognizing that as a rhetorician he was concerned with no more than the normal, the ordinary, the probable.

This reference to a specific example of Sterne's rhetoric is to indicate one peculiar application of certain traditional rhetorical theories; the theories discussed following, therefore, are intended to define rhetoric both in the abstract and in Sterne's particular practice.

## 3. The Continuity of Rhetorical Theory

"I must acknowledge," Campbell apologized, almost subverting himself at the very introduction to his *Philosophy of Rhetoric* (1776), "that, as

far as I have been able to discover, there has been little improvement
in the theory of rhetoric made by the moderns. The observations and
rules transmitted to us as from . . . Aristotle, Cicero, and Quintilian,
have been for the most part only translated by later critics, or put into
modish dress and new arrangement." His excuse for his own produc-
tion, besides a modish dress and new arrangement,[7] was that the psychology of human nature, which pertains to the pathetic proofs of
rhetoric, had recently arrived at new refinements, as evidenced in a
more general application in Lord Kames's *Elements of Criticism*. This
regard for what Locke would consider the weaker, because nonrational,
faculties of men is probably an evidence of the sensibility which was the
*dernier cri* of the period; nevertheless, considered in the rhetorical
tradition it is only a reëmphasis of the classical philosophy of rhetoric
long out of mode among the general laity and proper clergy, a search
of the circumstances which can energize standard attitudes and prejudices. Hume so fondly delighted in this view of ancient rhetoric that he
wrote an essay "Of Eloquence" (1742), not only lamenting the pale
colors of modern oratory, but even proposing a return to classical
techniques.

> It may be pretended that the decline of eloquence is owing to the superior
> good sense of the moderns, who reject with disdain all those rhetorical tricks,
> employed to seduce the judges, and will admit of nothing but solid argument in
> any debate or deliberation . . . But I see no reason why it should make them
> despair absolutely. . . . It should make them redouble their art.

Sterne's pulpit oratory was as full of rhetorical tricks as Hume could
have wished, had he wished for a pulpit oratory at all, and Cowper
allowed that if any rhetoric could save souls, Sterne's could.[8] Banish
these tricks as the previous half century had, and what is left is the
typical commonsense eighteenth-century sermon—or an early sermon
by Sterne. While Sterne's homiletic style was quite his own, it obviously
developed from a rhetorical practice older than the contemporary
"plain style"; it developed from a tradition which used catalogues of
ornaments and stratagems.[9] The decline of rhetorical strategy Sterne
turns to account in the elaborately wrought picture of Dr. Slop's offi-
cious dive into his green satchel, at the moment of catastrophe above-
stairs, for the instrument by which he alone can manipulate Tristram
into the world. Slop is about to make rhetorical use of the bag by draw-

ing from it, with a flourish, the forceps, the accoucheur's Excalibur, when he fumbles his rhetoric away. He was within an ace, says Tristram, of reviving a singular stroke of the eloquence of Athens and Rome, which consisted of effecting a peripety by sudden revelation of a dramatic fact secreted, say, within the folds of the toga. "All which plainly shews, may it please your worships, that the decay of eloquence, and the little good service it does at present, both within, and without doors, is owing to nothing else in the world but short coats, and the disuse of trunk-hose." [3.14.185–186.] Those ancients had bags for their tricks.

Nevertheless, while the *basic* theory of rhetoric does not change, rhetorical practice does, and changes in practice are confused with theory. Obviously, the rhetoric of Cicero is not the rhetoric of, say, Donne's poetry. Yet both satisfy what is basic in rhetorical theory. Furthermore, partial theories of rhetoric appear, peculiar to an individual or an age. In fact, steadfast confusions appear whenever the term "rhetoric" is considered, and have, in the course of nature, multiplied the critical stock on the subject into libraries. Is thought separable from ornament? and, indeed, what is ornament? How does logic differ from rhetoric, and rhetoric from nonoratorical prose? Since all the classical rhetoricians are concerned with oratory, what relation does their theory bear to other genres? What is the end of rhetoric? If it is persuasion, why were the Renaissance poets so consumed by rhetorical forms? And finally, what is the relation of theory to practice? When Shakespeare called for a "heaven of invention," it came somehow to him alone of all men—but probably not from Ramus's famous Renaissance treatise on logical invention. Where the author is more than a gerund-grinder (Sterne's label), rhetorical practice is always a function of personality, no matter how set be the manuals of his education. The Art of Sinking, Pope knew, requires a mechanical genius, and such a genius if he have a rhetoric is never without his tools; to read through the general run of rhetorical manuals is to strike up a real intimacy with the most perfectly blunted souls that the whole tradition of pseudocriticism can provide. There is nothing, says Pope, so great that a mechanical genius, prompted by laudable zeal, is not able to lessen it. And the basic conceptions of rhetorical theory are great: to come at a definition of "rhetoric" which includes these fundamental ideas we can do no better than to repeat the theory of Aristotle.

## 4. An Aristotelian Definition of Rhetoric

"Rhetoric" does not mean a copia of figures, or a style, or an ornate dissimulation. The most basic ideas of rhetoric, Aristotle's premises, are two: First, it is "the faculty of discerning in every case the available means of persuasion." It is the neutral art, indifferent to subject or attitude.[10] Secondly, the assumptions of its reasoning are concerned with probable human reactions. This is its distinction from dialectic, the discovery of near-necessary connections, regardless of the respondent.[11] Dialectic, in distinction to rhetoric, often approaches pure logic. For Aristotle, rhetoric is an art of appearances, though "appearances" need not imply duplicity; social business is its province. It recognizes the principles of predictable human conduct. Why people do not behave as they reason they should, of course is one of philosophers' favorite conundrums; and rhetoric exploits but does not attempt to solve the problem. From Socrates' decision that rhetoric is "mere cookery," the history of rhetorical theory is marked by periodic outcries against sophistry and appeals to emotion.[12] Locke is one such mark, and Sterne's comments on Locke are a reversion to the main current of rhetorical theory as the neutral art. Rhetorical treatises must always deal with this problem first of all, if they deal with theory at all (most of the Renaissance rhetorics were wholly practical). For example, the *Dialogues sur l'éloquence* of Fénelon[13] (Locke's contemporary), a treatise which certainly might have been to Sterne's taste since it spoke against scholastic and ecclesiastical subtleties in the pulpit and recommended a flap upon the heart and imagination, answers the charge that "l'éloquence . . . peut être prise . . . comme un art indifférent dont les méchants se peuvent servir aussi bien que les bons, et que peut persuader l'erreur, l'injustice, autant que la justice et la vérité . . .": "l'éloquence d'un méchant homme est bonne en elle-même; mais la fin à laquelle il la rapporte est pernicieuse." Locke's fulminations against rhetoric, "that instrument of deceit," show either that he did not comprehend Aristotle's philosophy of rhetoric, or that he believed the rhetorical practice of his time to be so decadent as to need more than objective, logical discussion, to need, in fact, rhetorical depreciation. Sterne's nature could not have allowed him to be deceived by this false cry: "an illustration is no argument [in logic],—nor do I maintain the wiping of a looking-glass clean, to be a syllogism;—but you all, may it please your worships, see the better for it . . ." [3.20.193]. Quintilian solves the problem by defining rhetoric as "ars dicendi bene," "so that a true orator must be, above all, a good man."[14] But Quintilian was a schoolteacher, and by "true orator" he meant the well-educated man, perfected in science and morals; he recognized the problem of the indifferent morality of rhetoric and simply avoided it, philosophically speaking. Perhaps for this reason so many subsequent rhetoricians lost sight of theory and merely restated the mechanics of the art.

Now if we consider again the implications of Aristotle's two premises (that rhetoric is the neutral art and that its arguments are concerned with predictable or probable human behavior), we may see why rhetorical method afforded Sterne such artistic energy.[15] Aristotle's *Rhetoric* is not an *a priori* system; it is a theory based upon observation. The flyleaf of the Sir Richard Jebb translation[16] quotes an appreciation of the *Rhetoric* by Edward Copleston, Bishop of Llandaff, descriptive of this observation:

> The Treatise on Rhetoric is a magazine of intellectual riches. . . . The author's principles are the result of extensive original induction. He sought them, if ever man did seek them, in the living pattern of the human heart. All the recesses and windings of that hidden region he has explored: all its caprices and affections—whatever tends to excite, to ruffle, to amuse, to gratify, or to offend it—have been carefully examined. The reason of these phenomena is demonstrated, the method of creating them is explained. . . . The whole is a text-book of human feeling; a storehouse of taste; an exemplar of condensed and accurate, but uniformly clear and candid reasoning.

A textbook of human feeling, not of logic on the one hand or of private sentiment on the other. Aristotle's study then is of types: he details desires and affections, still quite recognizable. For example:

> . . . men are angry with those who slight them before five classes of people—(1) their rivals; (2) those whom they admire; (3) those by whom they wish to be admired; (4) those whom they revere; (5) those by whom they are revered . . .

> . . . we chastise more severely those [servants] who . . . deny the fault . . . [for] that denial . . . is shamelessness; and shamelessness is a kind of slighting and disdain; at least we feel no shame before those whom we greatly disdain.

> We like those who praise the good things which we possess and especially those which we fear we do not possess. . . . We like those who resemble us and have the same pursuits, provided that they do not thwart us, and that our livelihood does not come from the same source . . .

. . . pity is not felt by the utterly lost . . . nor by those who think themselves
supremely prosperous . . . pity is felt by those who are in the intermediate
states.[17]

There is no morality, per se, good or bad, in these analyses; they
are materials of the neutral art, indifferent to topic or attitude. They
constitute the material of ethical (appeal to the audience from the character of the speaker) and pathetic (appeal to the affections of the
audience) proofs. Logical proofs by rhetorical enthymeme are, says
Aristotle, not to be given in long chains, but worked in here and there.[18]
One would not put most pathetic appeals in the form of enthymemes,
since they act directly and not by ratiocination, *but even enthymemes
start with premises that depend upon probable human attitudes.*

In each form of proof, however, one thing is common: the regard
for the affections of the audience; truth is not an intrinsic consideration.
For rhetoric is, as Aristotle says, a kind of dialectic of contingencies.[19]
The effect of a good rhetoric must be, then, to maintain the audience in
a kinetic state, question and answer, demonstration and refutation,
logic and emotion, hyperbole and diminution, according to the dictates
of each emotion. Thought unfolds, turns and re-turns.[20] Necessarily
there must be an audience with time and inclination to endure this sort
of stimulus. Recognizing this, De Quincey, who had a real perception
of the theory of rhetoric, moodily reflected that rhetoric had passed
from modern Europe. "No rhetorician is likely to appear again," he
wrote. "It is a conscious art that requires either the introverted energies
of the monastic ages or a quiescent state of the public mind."[21]

## 5. *One Relation of Oratory to Rhetoric in Prose Fiction*

But De Quincey speaks of oratory, an art which in the classical conception was analogous in its larger-than-life techniques to the drama,
wherein emotions could be represented by declamation, by masks, by
the sock and buskin. This interrelationship is noted in the *Poetics,*
where Aristotle refers the poet to his *Rhetoric* for advice on framing
the characters' speeches.

The traditional association of oratory, with its grand devices and
structures proper for the mass appeals of the forum or theater, has never
been divorced from either rhetorical theory or practice. After all, if

rhetoric is a system for appealing to human norms, it necessarily is limited to broad strokes. It need not lack subtlety, but the subtlety lies in "trickery," not in elusive expression. The formalities of oratory: the five-part structure of exordium, narrative, confirmation, confutation, and peroration; the general topics of invention for argument; the syntactical rhythms; and the obvious construction of many figures—these formalities become infused into other genres, and with subtler effects: Rosamund Tuve has suggested the symbolic qualities which images developed from formal argumentation possess in Elizabethan and metaphysical poetry.[22] When Sydney's muse directs him to look into his heart and write, he is considering ways of getting material for the forms of invention because invention is a strategy to give pleasure (through fulfillment of form) to one's respondent. He is not talking about the writing of a poem, but about the larger matter of the stratagems men must use to persuade. As the irony of the *Beowulf* often derives from the extremes of contrast in the primitive language (the use of litotes, for example), so the contrasts between formal statement and a reference usually more intimately considered can lend an ironic or satiric tone. And of course the necessarily grand proportions of oratorical form easily turn, like hyperbole, that most insecure of all figures, to the work of humor and pathos when they descend from the rostrum to the petty forums of undressed life. (One might detail, for example, Dickens' rhetorical use of hyperbole for both pathos and humor.) The idea of declamation is easily associated with the idea of the "humours." And the pathos of such characters as Falstaff, Don Quixote, and Walter Shandy is bound up with their need of declaiming to a world that cannot quite hear their peculiar melodies. Indeed, the forms of persuasion as used by these characters have also a literal function as in genuine oratory—for each character *is* persuasive in his own right.

The very weight of inflated oratorical formalities in *Tristram Shandy* should make some of the so-called sentiment, the tears, for example, suspect. Not the moist glimmer of a tear teetering on an eyelid, but rather, fountains fraught with tears, is the stuff of oratory: "Sententious showers, O let them fall. Their cadence is Rhetoricall." Crashaw ("Upon the Death of a Gentleman") is not here striving after comedy; by reminding the reader of rhetoric, he wishes to symbolize the abandoned reactions of the forum. Literary historians who catch each

tear of *Tristram Shandy* (or, indeed, of *A Sentimental Journey)* to
exhibit as proof that they have found the wellspring of the sentimental
novel should take time to hear the cadences of a facetious rhetoric.
Consider here the pathetic statements overwrought to a kind of comedy
by rhetorical forms new-found in the boudoir.

REVENGE from some baneful corner shall level a tale of dishonour at thee,
which no innocence of heart or integrity of conduct shall set right.—The fortunes
of thy house shall totter,—thy character, which led the way to them, shall bleed
on every side of it,—thy faith questioned,—thy works belied,—thy wit forgotten,
—thy learning trampled on. To wind up the last scene of thy tragedy, CRUELTY
and COWARDICE, twin ruffians, hired and set on by MALICE in the dark, shall strike
together at all thy infirmities and mistakes . . .
Yorick scarce ever heard this sad vaticination of his destiny read over to him,
but with a tear stealing from his eye, and a promissory look attending it, that he
was resolved, for the time to come, to ride his tit with more sobriety.
[1.12.29–30]

Tears, rhetorical tears. And yet there is quite genuine emotion.
Sterne, like Shakespeare, knew the infallible receipt for pathetic comedy: a moving situation treated with rueful bombast. Yet, when Toby
puts his fly out the window, hardboiled critics choke on what they think
is sentiment. "Go—says he . . . I'll not hurt thee, . . . —I'll not
hurt a hair of thy head: Go, . . . go poor devil, get thee gone, why
should I hurt thee? This world surely is wide enough to hold both thee
and me." [2.12.113.] Bombast, rhetorical bombast, marked by ana-
phora (marked repetition) and ending with a sententia: "This world,
etc." Not surely a natural gambol of the man of feeling. Bombast is
seldom used with such delicacy in English comedy. A blatant beast like
Fluellen is its usual product. But Falstaff is nothing like Fluellen,
despite their sharing of the *miles gloriosus* label. Falstaff, a true rhetor,
is an obvious English suggestion for Sterne's characters.

Before leaving this matter of the crossing of oratorical forms with
prose fiction for the end of comedy, we may notice a similar use in
Rabelais. "Of the grief wherewith Gargantua was moved at the decease
of his wife Badebec"[23] we have the testimony of Rabelais's rhetorical
technique, the outsize strokes of which display at once the essential
comedy of the human need to experience the pathetic and yet to talk
oneself out of it.

When Pantagruel was born, there was none more astonished and perplexed
than his father Gargantua; for on the one side seeing his wife Badebec dead, and

on the other side his son Pantagruel born, so fair and so great, he knew not what
to say nor what to do: and the doubt that troubled his brain was to know whether
he should cry for the death of his wife, or laugh for the joy of his son. He was
*hinc indè* choked with sophistical arguments, for he framed them very well *in
modo et figura,* but he could not resolve them, remaining pestered and entangled
by this means, like a mouse caught in a trap or a kite snared in a gin. "Shall I
weep?" said he. "Yes. For why? My so good wife is dead, who was the most this,
the most that, that ever was in the world. Never shall I see her, never shall I
recover such another; it is unto me an inestimable loss! O my good God, what
had I done that thou shouldst thus punish me? . . . O false death, how injurious
and despiteful hast thou been to me! How malicious and outrageous have I found
thee in taking her from me, my well-beloved wife, to whom immortality did of
right belong." With these words he did cry like a cow, but on a sudden fell a-laugh-
ing like a calf . . .

Tears, rhetorical tears—before the sentimental novel was invented.
The parallel with Walter's dilemma upon the intelligence of his son
Bobby's death is obvious. He settles into his pleasure, oratory, the only
way he can express himself, and comes off, balancing woe and pleasure,
at least as well as he was before he heard the news.

## 6. *Rhetoric and Ornament*

The formal figures of oratory, called "ornament," are, of course, all set
out in the books of rhetoric, but they are rhetoric only so far as they
satisfy the basic aims of rhetoric. It is in his use of ornament that the
individual emerges and stands as a mark in the tradition. Now, Sterne
in his office of preacher considered himself a rhetorician, *not a theological lecturer;* he talks so much about the heart versus the head in
this activity that the standard commentator pounces on the phrase as
another evidence for installing Sterne as the priest, bating his impurities, of sentimentalism. But a casual inspection of Sterne's style shows
that the heartbeats are the peculiar rhythm of certain fairly repetitious
figures and tropes of word and sentence. Figures, of course, as many
or more than Quintilian knew, are to be found afresh in every morning's
newspaper, but the surely calculated pile of them that is Cicero's prose,
the bold-relief characters, crossed affections, and stentorian harmonies,
is the mark of the exigencies of the forum. In more intimate literary
genres rhetorical ornament has subtler functions, as suggested above,
but whether in oratory or prose fiction, it is the form of thought. For
example:

Walter's last philosophical oration, on the deed of darkness, is just begun with the statement of the problem, ". . . wherefore, when we go about to make and plant a man, do we put out the candle?" [9.33.645], when Tristram notes that Walter (like a rhetor true) "avails himself of the prolepsis." He proceeds to analysis by testimony, division, erotesis, comparison, enargia (vivid representation), and a battery of other figures. This is not merely burlesque: as it happens, prolepsis, which Tristram holds up for the reader's consideration and edification, as he does other rhetorical devices throughout the book, is not exclusively Walter's trick. The figure itself is a framing of a statement so as to pose questions or objections and anticipate them. "This figure," says Quintilian, "is akin to that known as communication, when we actually take our opponents into consultation." The raising of questions, sometimes by division of a topic, sometimes by insinuation or equivocation, and a mocking communication or deliberation with his respondents, is probably the characteristic device of Sterne's style. Either he means nothing more than burlesque of rhetoric and learning, or his characteristic figures are the form of his meaning. Without the formal figures, in fact, *Tristram* would be something like Locke's "I-know-not-what," that is, substance with all the accidents removed.

Still, "mere ornament," mere "figurative decoration," is something spoken of by historians of style as somehow separable from the substance of what is said. "Mere ornament" is said to have been the quality abstracted from style by the seventeenth-century reform of English prose. Richard F. Jones outlines this assault on the figurative style.[24] It is true that Hobbes, Cowley, Dryden, and Pope all took time out to ridicule figurative ornament. But if figures, as has been suggested from Sterne's use, are really inseparable from meaning, how can we understand this sudden assault on the figurative style? The answer seems to be that the seventeenth century, reflecting upon Renaissance excrescences, became aware of the complications and snares implicit in the use of oratorical forms in alien genres. On the one hand the bathetic, as Pope noticed, is very easily obtained where the pathetic is aimed for, and on the other the problems of symbolism and irony must be recognized in the use of very formal structures. Furthermore, the new ideals of science and a strictly regulated pattern of society made exposition more important than persuasion. The seventeenth century, Morris Croll writes,[25] regarded the history of prose style as a story of relations and conflicts between two modes of style—oratorical and essay. And the period was interested in the essay, and, in the pulpit, in a dispassionate moral exposition. The attack on figures and extreme formalism is really an attack on oratory, oratory often ludicrously misplaced—in prose contexts demanding informality, and in a Church no longer interested in emotional suasion. The "reform" of prose style is, then, not really an attempt to separate figures from meaning, but a statement that the style of oratory expresses meanings not useful to the age. Swift is often held as the special triumph of the plain style, but Swift merely used *his* characteristic ornament, the various figures that express irony, to the exclusion of other ornament. Sterne, too, used *his* characteristic figures, those expressing communication, equivocation, and paradox, almost to the exclusion of other ornament.

W. K. Wimsatt is undoubtedly correct in the premise for his study *The Prose Style of Samuel Johnson*,[26] that "rhetorical devices ought to be considered no more artificial than sentences," but it is difficult to find evidence that this is, as he says, a seventeenth-century idea, or that "ancient rhetorians all seem to see style as something apart from meaning." Indeed, it was not a real question to them. They all speak of style by using the term "ornament," to be sure, but if we consider that the real purpose of rhetoric, for them, was to affect the dispositions of the audience, "ornament" becomes the very form of that purpose.

The connection of classical rhetorical theory with "ornament" is so intimate that to predicate a separation of meaning from style is a mere exercise of words. The dynamic of testing the responses of the audience is carried by ornament. Cicero in two pages catalogues the forms (that is, figures) of this dynamic:

. . . our whole style of oratory is to be distinguished and frequently interspersed with brilliant lights, as it were, of thoughts and words. For the *dwelling* on a single circumstance has often a considerable effect; and a clear *illustration* and *exhibition* of matters to the eye of the audience, almost as if they were transacted before them. This has wonderful influence in giving a representation of any affair, both to illustrate what is represented, and to amplify it, so that the point which we amplify may appear to the audience to be really as great as the powers of our language can represent it. Opposed to this is *rapid transition* over a thing, which may often be practiced. There is also *signification* that more is to be understood than you have expressed; . . . and *extenuation,* and, what borders upon this, *ridicule* . . . and *digression* from the subject, and when gratification has thus been afforded, the return to the subject ought to be happy and elegant; *proposition* of what you are about to say, *transition* from what has been said, and *retrogression;* there is *repetition;* apt *conclusion* of reasoning; *exaggeration,* or surpassing of the truth, for the sake of amplification or diminution; *interrogation,* and, akin to this, as it were, *consultation* or seeming inquiry, followed by the delivery of your own opinion; and *dissimulation,* the *humor* of saying one thing and signifying another, which steals into the minds of men in a peculiar manner, and which is extremely pleasing when it is well managed, not in a vehement strain of language, but in a conversational style; also *doubt;* and *distribution;* and *correction* of yourself, either before or after you have said a thing, or when you repel anything from yourself; there is also *premonition,* with regard to what you are going to prove; . . . *imitation* of manners and character, either with names of persons or without, which is a great ornament to a speech, and adapted to conciliate the feelings even in the utmost degree, and often also to rouse them; the *introduction of fictitious characters,* the most heightened figure of exaggeration; there is *description; falling into a willful mistake;* . . . *anticipation; comparison* and *example,* two figures which have a very great effect; *division;* . . . *anger; reproach; promise; deprecation; beseeching;* slight *deviation* from your intended course, but not like digression, which I mentioned before; *expurgation; conciliation; attack; wishing; execration.* Such are the figures with which thoughts give lustre to a speech.[27]

Transition, ridicule, digression, retrogression, amplification, interrogation, dissimulation, doubt, consultation, correction. Run down with his variegated fancy, with his genius for sudden shifts at the moment of maximum tension, this catalogue is the very course of Sterne's technique. And, incidentally, the rapid shuffling of the figures of interrogation, doubt, consultation, and correction makes that quality of his style which, though never heard in conversation, is often called "conversational." For example:

. . . now as these words cost nothing, I long from my soul to tell the reader what they are; but here is the question—they must be told him plainly, and with the most distinct articulation, or it will answer no end—and yet to do it in that plain way—though their reverences may laugh at it in the bed-chamber—full well I wot, they will abuse it in the parlour: for which cause, I have been volving and revolving in my fancy some time, but to no purpose, by what clean device or facete contrivance I might so modulate them, that whilst I satisfy *that ear* which the reader chuses to *lend* me—I might not dissatisfy the other which he keeps to himself.

—My ink burns my finger to try—and when I have—'twill have a worse consequence—it will burn (I fear) my paper.

—No;—I dare not—

But if you wish to know how the *abbess* of *Andoüillets,* and a novice of her convent got over the difficulty (only first wishing myself all imaginable success) —I'll tell you without the least scruple. [7.20.503–504]

The life of a writer is warfare between himself and the reader. This is the technique of rhetoric.

There is much that could be quoted from Aristotle, Cicero, and Quintilian in support of the necessity of ornament to effect the end of rhetoric—to find the available means of persuasion,—but a recent consideration of the matter by Craig La Drière, "Rhetoric and 'Merely Verbal' Art,"[28] makes, it would seem, a final and definitive summary. La Drière begins where most rhetorical theorists have ended—with the historical fact of the continually expressed opposition between *res* and *verba*. His analysis explains both the opposition and the constant connection of rhetoric with forms and figures: ". . . all through the history of rhetoric there runs the opposition of words and things, *res* and *verba*. The conflict between them is in practice the conflict between 'philosophy' and 'poetry' which Plato said was an ancient thing in his time; we should say rather, . . . between 'science' and 'literature.' . . . Actually what is called *merely verbal* may not be directly verbal expression at all, but some property of what is expressed, affectivity as distinguished from intellectuality, feeling as distinct from thought, or even one kind of thought or reality as distinct from another." La Drière reminds us of De Quincey's insight: rhetoric is a game, in which the writer and his reader contract to go through certain motions as certain springs are touched. An erotesis may be quite as affirmative as an affirmation, but it demands something extra from the audience, it demands that we start a quarrel with ourselves and resolve it in the affirmative. This we perform dutifully if the orator has any skill at all. We are easily led by forms. In Sterne's figures of paradox and communication, for example, as in an unresolved chord, we demand fulfillment of the form. Per se, a verbal form is just as respectable as, and no less substantial than, a dramatic form. Ornament deserves the honor in verbal structures that, say, peripeteia demands in dramatic. In specific instances any form, verbal or dramatic, may or may not become its possibility.

Since rhetoric is only concerned with insecure probabilities, it differs from pure dialectic which depends upon a close approximation to depersonalized, abstract truth, with no regard of the auditor. Rhetoric must depend upon the auditor; hence its subsidiary dependence upon psychology and figures. Ultimately, probability, the criterion of rhetorical proof, means the probability of the auditor's reactions to any given stimulus. Walter, a facet of Sterne as surely as is Yorick or Tristram, and not a mere burlesque figure, had, we remember, "the elements of rhetoric and logic so blended up in him" as to give him "a shrewd guess at the weaknesses and passions of his respondent," for "he could argue on either side of a question." This is a fair statement of the aim of rhetoric, and the description might well be applied to Sterne the preacher, or to Sterne the perverse moralist in *Tristram Shandy*. His conflict with Locke is part of the moral of *Tristram,* for Locke's confusion is that he failed to recognize, as had Aristotle, that rhetoric cannot be the art of deceit, since it does not pretend to abstract truth. The rhetorician may be moral or immoral, but rhetoric is neither the one nor the other.

# CHAPTER FIVE • *"Tristram Shandy's"*
# *Holy Beginnings*

WRITING her cousin Elizabeth Montagu to solicit business and publicity for the posthumous sermons of Mr. Yorick, Lydia Sterne took nice care to establish her own character as surety for their excellence.[1] With some acumen, she described herself as having "not the least grain" of her father's wit ("We both [i.e., mother and daughter] thought it an unhappy turn in my father"), but "some gentlemen" had told her that the sermons were "very good ones." The "good ones" were heralded by Sterne himself as "the sweepings of the Author's study after his death."[2] Lydia's plentiful lack of wit could not have noticed why her collection constituted the "sweepings." For the main part the sermons of Sterne's own publication (Vols. I–IV) are the witty (though not very) and Shandean ones. They were first advertised to the world in *Tristram Shandy,* and one of them, "The Abuses of Conscience Considered," is an integral part of the book. In Lydia's group the purloined platitudes are usually little altered, merely stolen goods. Sterne admitted it. "The sermon upon the jewish dispensation—I don't like it at all; . . . 'tis all tritical . . . For this sermon I shall be hanged,—for I have stolen the greatest part of it. Doctor Paidagunes found me out. ☞ Set a thief to catch a thief." [6.11.427.] There is a distinction between these tritical sermons and the Shandean. The latter are a rhetorical concoction of interrogative devices intended to test the conflict of different attitudes and affections in the auditors. They are, in Sterne's use of the word, dramatic. [2.17.141.]

"He is a great master of the pathetic," Cowper wrote to a friend, "and if that or any other species of rhetoric could renew the human heart and turn it from the power of Satan unto God, I know no writer better qualified to make proselytes to the cause of virtue than Sterne. But, alas! . . . "³ Cowper does not mean by "the pathetic" that they trade on pity, tenderness, or sorrow, but rather the pathetic "proof" of traditional rhetorical theory. That is, persuasion by appeals to the affections or mores of the audience. Probably this is what Sterne meant by that private cliché of his, "more from the heart than from the head."

This chapter is a digression in order to suggest by way of noting the holy beginnings of *Tristram* that Sterne was never really out of the preacher's habit.

We know that Sterne was able to compose in the Shandean style as early as 1750, the date of "The Abuses of Conscience Considered," a sermon later to be delivered by Trim. On the other hand there is no reason at all to believe, as has been suggested by some critics, that some of the Shandean sermons were a product of *Tristram,* that Sterne, realizing his strike, composed these sermons for the trade.⁴

A most marked product of the Shandean vein, "The House of Feasting and the House of Mourning Described," Sterne recommended to his daughter in France as "one of the best."⁵ Certainly the sermons of its type were his most valued ones. Valued by Sterne, Yorick, Walter, Toby, and even Slop, not as art but as homiletic [2.17.141]. We must remember that Walter is at times to be taken as seriously as the "lousy prebendary" of York Minster, for he delivers Sterne's sermon, "Trust in God,"⁶ after Dr. Slop's forceps have broken down Tristram's nose.* And interpolating remarks of Toby, in his antithetical role, make of Walter's oratory a dialectic rhetoric in exactly the manner of the best Shandean sermons, where *Sterne plays the roles* of differing attitudes.

It is interesting to speculate how the hearts awaiting Mr. Sterne's

---

*See discussion below, chap. vi, p. 117.

weekly flap in York Cathedral or Sutton Church may have bent their
sensibilities to the Shandean task at hand. By following the appeals of
several of the sermons, we can understand what the auditor was up
against. He might first have to juggle an opening conundrum which
would sound profane in an institution whose indigenous riddles were
all long ago carefully classified. Sterne at the outset made his texts a
nervous charge: *"It is better to go to the house of mourning than to the
house of feasting.* [Ecclesiastes, 7:2]—That I deny . . ."⁷ *"And it
came to pass in those days, . . . that there was a certain Levite . . .
who took unto him a concubine.* [Judges 19:1.]—A concubine!"⁸ *"For
we trust we have a good conscience.* [Hebrews 3:18.]—Trust!"⁹

But this sort of thing is not simply fanfare for the "one Bellows
Blower, three singing men, one Vicar, and one Residentiary," whom
Sterne records as his entire audience on one occasion in York Minster.
It was part of his system of thinking, the system which later formed
*Tristram Shandy.*

"That I deny—but let us hear the wise man's reasoning upon it—
*for that* is *the end of all men, and the living* will *lay it to* his *heart: sorrow
is better than laughter*—for a crack'd-brain'd order of Carthusian
monks, I grant, but not for men of the world." Ecclesiastes equals
monkery equals crack'd-brain'dness. Then an erotesis, "For what purpose, do you imagine, has GOD made us?" Society or the Sierra Morena?
With this allusion, the preacher, still in the pulpit, invokes *Don Quixote*
and all its ridicule. A series of divisions of the first erotesis, all interrogative. We are on a Quixotic "road" of life, sallying forth after sad
accidents. Then a long list, in contrast, of the fair charms of life provided by the Best of Beings, who, perhaps, *barely* gets the nod in the
argument so far. But the question is still with us, how did Ecclesiastes
get so stupidly confounded?

But by the next paragraph the auditor is told that he is undiscrimi-
nating, should not have asked the question. "I will not contend at
present against this rhetorick . . . ," for, it seems, there is a distinction of some sort. The audience is twitted: this is only rhetoric, after
all. We may take the pleasures along the highway, only if we *are* going
somewhere. This is about as far as this road simile can decently go
without bogging into comedy. Already we have had to take *Don Quixote*
with a solemn face. Now: "But let us not lose sight of the argument in

pursuit of the simile." We have been warned of rhetoric; now we are warned of the simile which supposedly overthrows rhetoric. Finally, then, there is a conventional interpretation of Solomon's injunction: we are merely to keep in mind the House of Mourning as a balance for the wiles of the Tempter. This is the full force of the Wise Man's words, but "I will endeavour to bring the subject still nearer." Into the House of Feasting.

"Imagine then such a house  . . .  " Two sexes, shopworn escapist sentiments, hearts open, fermenting blood, commerce between sexes, heart passages unguarded, music, caressing looks, singing men, violin, lute. Folly may be in the room. He may traffic with the imagination. Look for him. But this description is not true; it is saying the worst. But maybe it *is* true. And so into the House of Mourning. O God! Broken hearts, limbs, bodies, souls. Look and beware. But—not for the love of bewaring. Beware of that.

There is nothing profane in the riddles after all, there are no jests. And yet there *is* a sort of mocking of the auditor, a pious rally, surely, but how far can it go within the bounds of Church decorum? And do even a dozen turns of affections, each a comment on the others, constitute a good sermon?

Such kittenish mocking of affections is ever on the verge of comedy, and the real value of Sterne's rhetoric is that in ideal form it produces a real delicacy of intuition as one affection measures another. In ideal form it is a skeptical comedy. However, skepticism that remains religious produces ultimately either stoicism or dogmatism—or both. If it is arrested by theological conventions and Sterne's sort of sentimentalism, a continual war is assured in which the affirmation can go no further than the skeptical mind will allow. Sterne could make a comedy with Locke's philosophy, but Church doctrine allowed only vapid ingenuity. On the sexual topic alone we can see this contrast. In "The House of Feasting," sex is a submerged theme, with Folly leering and kicking it up now and then. But the warning is for those who are not fortified mentally against temptation; there may be others "of so pure and chaste a turn of mind—that the house of feasting, with all its charms and temptations, was never able to excite a thought, or awaken an inclination which virtue need to blush at . . ." Irony? We know from *Tristram Shandy* that Sterne did not believe anything like this. Tristram uses the same rhetorical techniques to excite thoughts and awaken inclinations which "virtue" (equals hypocrisy now) *must* blush at. The same statement in *Tristram,* Sterne would do everything possible to show as ironic. The inventions on sex in *Tristram* are endless and conceptual (not prurient or corrupt; the sermon is more open to that charge). He was ruled by some censorship in *Tristram* ("Swift has said a hundred things I durst not say—unless I was Dean of St. Patrick's"), but not much ("the very idea [of my coat's color] in my head would render my book not worth a groat")[10] What in the book *is* simply sniggering (and I think there is some but not much) is probably attributable to that censorship, just as the banal allusions to sex in "The House of Feasting" result from the impossibility of his rhetoric's functioning freely in the realm of theology. His inclinations were worldly, adjusted to the mean, and best expressed in comedy.

In one Shandean sermon, "The Levite and His Concubine," sex is an overt rhetorical topic, but even here the real theme, prudery, is arrested, before it can become meaningful, by an etymological quibble which saves the day for propriety—after propriety has already been subverted. Even so, the topic gets good Shandean invention before it is abruptly deadened by the purifying quibble.

> *And it came to pass in those days, when there was no king in Israel, that there was a certain Levite sojourning on the side of mount Ephraim, who took unto him a concubine.*
>
> A concubine!—but the text accounts for it, *"for in those days there was no king in Israel,"* and the Levite, you will say, like every other man in it, did what was right in his own eyes,—and so, you may add, did his concubine too—*for she played the whore against him, and went away.*—

Dr. Slop, defending the True Faith, instantly poohed Walter's praise of Yorick's sermon as dramatic eloquence, "We preach much in that way with us." But, said Slop (now really Mr. Yorick in ironical costume), "we never introduce any character into them below a patriarch or a patriarch's wife, or a martyr or a saint" [2.17.141].[11] Sterne had no traffic with saints, and martyrs, he knew, were not of his stripe. Low comedy was his forte. A concubine!, for example. In this exordium there is first an appeal to prudery from the moral quality of the word and punctuation. But then an invention on cause: way of the world—after all, people will be people. Appeal to righteous authority. Dash, and change of viewpoint. Humph, says Prudery, he got what he deserved, a whore. A whore, censure is deserved; and in lofty stentorian tones: "—Then shame and grief go with her, and wherever she seeks a shelter, may the hand of justice shut the door against her." This sudden ironic change of "voice" or character, labeled by rhetoricians "prosopopoeia," is one of Sterne's most characteristic forms of style in *Tristram*.

Next paragraph reverses character again. This is a dialectical argument with all characters comprehended in the speaker. "Not so," says the new character, a cynical fellow, to that righteous prude just gone off-stage after spitting his malediction. Not so, look here, she went home and was received as a daughter. Dash, enter new character, a moralist: "Blessed interval for the Levite to meditate and thank God for his deliverance." The cynic goes back to the task. Unfortunately the old man did not meditate at all; he got his ass out and chased after her. Utter confusion by this time; here is the Bible not making things come out RIGHT. The whore goes home, her chastity gone, but still unchastened, the cuckold is at her side, the father, who was supposed to say "Never darken my door," receives both of them with open arms.

And now for his first entrance, Yorick the preacher of a dozen voices, in a sardonic inflection: "A most sentimental group! you'll say: [change of inflection] and so it is, my good commentator, the world talks of everything: give but the outlines of a story,—let spleen or prudery snatch the pencil, and they will finish it . . . with so dirty a colouring, that candour and courtesy will sit in torture as they look at it." What might be the palliating causes of the concubine's concubinage? A dozen suggestions, and the auditor begins to suspect that morality is about to be banished by a Feeling Heart. But perhaps compassion can go too far, the preacher suggests. An apostrophic appeal to authority, "O Abraham," if this was wrong why didst thou have so many concubines? and Solomon, "wise—deluded," three hundred!

This is the point of ultimate complication, even the Bible is impeached. Contraries are already set out, paradox is conceived, and all affections brought into a tension. Unfortunately the denouement, the untying of the knot, is less stimulating. A *Deus ex etymologia* saves the concubine from concubinage. The word, it seems, in its primitive Hebrew sense means almost the same as "wife," implying a social shadow but not a legal one. As for God, he can suspend his own rules:

that accounts for Abraham and Solomon. And charity can restore to
the concubine her chastity; she was a hapless wanderer, sweet in her
sorrow. The horrid catastrophe of the Bible story is omitted. This is a
fair sermon, but the complications used to excite and cross affections
are too poignant for the purpose, which is only to discredit rash judgment. (Actually they are not far from bathos or buffoonery.) Sterne's
rhetoric can create an emotional impasse, but theological decorum
prevents an escape. The motives of *Tristram Shandy* have not the onus
of religious and moral mystery to prevent their resolution.

The broad structure of warring affections is clear. He had a feeling
for standard reactions and he knew what Quixotic drama lay in the
sallies of one cliché against another.

Whatever figures serve to make the audience partisan, Sterne uses
with abandon. "The Prodigal Son" is a useful guide to these figures.
So repetitious are they that a sort of rhythm of effects is created which
itself is a form and which permits the audience to play the game, just
as the spectator of drama plays the game of stage conventions. An
irony mixes with homiletic in these sermons, the irony of self-contem-
plation. The audience must have consciousness of its own participation,
by way of the figure of "communication," in the various forms of deliberating, doubting, asking questions to which the answer is obvious—
or better, impossible,—asking and answering in sequence, anticipation
of objections, and asking questions through the person of a feigned
speaker (prosopopoeia).

"The Prodigal Son" opens with aporia (doubting), a dubious salute
to the auditor: "I know not whether the remark is to our honour or
otherwise, that lessons of wisdom have never such power over us, as
when they are wrought into the heart, through the groundwork of a
story which engages the passions." Then a deliberation which leaves the
auditor no choice but to deflate himself: "Is it that we are like iron and
must first be heated before we can be wrought upon? or, Is the heart
so in love with deceit, that where a true report will not reach it, we must
cheat it with a fable, in order to come at the truth?" We are given the
process of rhetoric to consider in relation to ourselves; we must review
our sensitivity for the work to come. Next, another figure of doubting;
we are told that the question is not even pertinent. Negative conciliation.
End exordium. There then follows such a division of the Bible's account

as the heart all atremble might invent: life, fortune, virtue, temptation, pleasure, knowledge, evil knowledge, women, charm, poison—the heart pitches around in this indecorous manner with no grammatical connectives save dashes. The rhetorical figure is asyndeton, supposed to indicate agitation, but, as Sterne uses it, asyndeton is the standard method for gathering complications, perfectly analogous to his other devices for fracturing ideas and affections, the shifts in character, attitude, tone, and subject matter. Well, the answer to all this commotion, as we might expect, having met Sterne before, is only one line away. "The dissuasive would but inflame his desire." Rhetoric is concerned with normal motives.

Now the Prodigal, his furniture in order, struggles to restrain himself for his father's farewell tears. "I see the picture," says Sterne. (The rhetorician's figure, picturing, to illustrate ideas.) The picture is a study in contraries, as are all of Sterne's pictures (in *Tristram,* e.g., Walter and Trim orating simultaneously on the death of Bobby, the manner of the one exactly opposite to that of the other). While in the foreground the elder brother holds the Prodigal's hand, unwilling to let it go, on one side of the canvas the loaded camels already slipping away. The Prodigal's forced sedateness struggling against his perfect joy and the father's perfect despair. The preacher changes to the character of the father (prosopopoeia), breaks into an apostrophe. "The apostrophe," says Quintilian, "is a mark of violent emotion." But in Sterne's personal rhetoric it has another function: it serves as one more contrary, in this case, of tone. Here it isolates the picture *as a figure. (The audience must not forget that this is rhetoric;* it has been reminded from the opening sentence.) But we have no more than reached the apex of this apostrophe when the preacher tells us, "We will seek no further than this idea." We have been given already cause enough for invention. These tricks, the preacher suggests, are indecently easy for the rhetor. The end of the rhetoric here comes perilously close to being simply an appreciation of the power of rhetoric.

Sterne has another set of characters, put on in *Tristram* more often than in the sermons, acting a sort of dumbshow. These are the personifications, usually of affections, *gemütlich* characters, most of them. Pleasures solicit the Prodigal, the Soul retires and sits pensive, after his distress Compassion tells a story in three words, the Heart is in love

with Deceit, Affections play with each other. In "The Abuses of Conscience," Conscience is no less than a scampish Ambidexter, the Vice
of an old Morality, his spirit, like that of chopfallen Yorick, new-found
in eighteenth-century York Minster. We are never very far from *Tristram Shandy's* errant scoundrel Gravity; or Desire, with vest held up
to the knee, snatching at Fancy; or Death who stops to hear Tristram's
joke and leaves, forgetting his commission. Personification, a form of
prosopopoeia, is described in most rhetorics as a very energetic device
of the pathetic, and proper for the high style or sublime. Again Sterne
works another contrary—a device reserved primarily for the sublime
or high style is modified by a homely application to a *slight,* but not
entire, sense of irony by which the auditor understands that he is not to
experience the sublime, but only to contemplate its effects. In *Tristram,*
similarly but more usefully, the devices of the sublime are seen as genuine pathetic on the level of the sympathetic characters, absorbed as
they are in themselves, but as irony from any view outside their
concerns. The sermons just escape this sort of pathetic comedy.

I have not meant to argue that the sermons, though dull, perhaps,
are unworthy of the pulpit (dullness is next to piety), or that they are
not perfectly serious. Rather, I would hope that the argument might go
the other way and indicate the seriousness of *Tristram Shandy* as a work
of rhetorical disputation. At any rate it is clear that while Sterne was not
perfectly suited for the ministry he nevertheless owed the Church a
great debt: it first permitted (perhaps forced) him to express himself.
It led him to his private rhetoric through the forms of tradition.

# CHAPTER SIX · *The Rhetoric of Self-Consciousness*

OFTEN the texture of Sterne's comedy is so perfectly delicate that such extremities as death itself (four deaths occur and one awaits the final word, in *Tristram*), or a cruel forceps delivery, or a ghastly wound, even an inadvertent circumcision, slide into the consciousness with not the slightest jar to our sensibilities. Low subjects become so formalized that what should be the crudest incongruity only adjusts the scales ever more nicely. It would seem hard for a poor but honest reader, for example, to consider euphorically an incident the nub of which is circumcision by a crashing sash window, but it is just another Shandean oddity that the operation only creates a fine sense of well-being. Hear Tristram's compassionate understanding and the chambermaid's gentle voice (even her sentence structure is nice) telling us the entire calamity:

> 'Twas nothing . . .
> O 'twould provoke a stone, to see how things are carried on in this world!—
> The chamber-maid had left no ******* *** under the bed:—Cannot you contrive, master, quoth Susannah, lifting up the sash with one hand, as she spoke, and helping me into the window seat with the other,—cannot you manage, my dear, for a single time to **** *** ** *** ******?

107

I was five years old.—Susannah did not consider that nothing was well hung in our family,—so slap came the sash down like lightening upon us;—nothing is left,—cried Susannah,—nothing is left—for me, but to run my country.— [5.17.376]

Thus with no prelude or preparation we hear of this incremental woe in Tristram's life. This is all. 'Twas nothing. Nothing of course happens to Susannah; scarcely anything happens to Tristram. The floating voices themselves are charmed by their vagrant world; their accents are infinitely benignant. They are so because existence, accidental though it be, is so preciously balanced in this Shandean world. One fortuitous motive merely brings an equal and opposite one into play. Why is the incident important? Because it permits the final fillip, a "bitter Philippick" on chambermaids, in Walter's slow rhetoric in the Tristrapaedia. And allows Walter a long harangue on divine mysteries, particularly *de subjecto circumcisionis* (and reminds us of the urgency of ritual to an eighteenth-century squire as well as to the ancient and noble savages of Asia Minor), allows Yorick to lecture (out of Rabelais) on polemic divines, Trim to say his religious and military catechism by rote, Walter to divide the mystical secrets of health, with the aid of ancient authorities, which engenders his engine of auxiliary verbs to enlarge Tristram's mind in compensation for the deprivation in other quarters. Why did the window drop? Because Trim had confiscated all the sashweights for war material, which fact allows Toby to dramatize ("Scarce exceeded by the invention of a dramatic writer") his own culpability as military superior to Trim. Every motive of the book instantly appears and, freshly energized, all is as it was.

Whatever happens in this world, the perpetual-motion machinery whirs on with perfect recollection, reminding us of all time, all customs, all motives, compounded in a four-mile circle of Yorkshire, a universal, if worldly, dialectic without end. There can be no catastrophe to this story, nothing can happen, simply because it is the rhetorical dialectical process, not progress, we watch. Were it not for the dozens upon dozens of references to the formalities of rhetoric in the text, were it not for Sterne's constantly reminding us of his power to engage and provoke us, the very delicacy of the cross-play of motives, affections, and logics in this ever-balanced world would suggest a skilled rhetor interested in the works rather than the end of rhetoric. As he subverted Locke, so

Sterne perverted quite self-consciously the devices of rhetorical persuasion so that they became personal and private stratagems to express his conception.

And since he, himself, makes so much of his rhetorical tricks in the book, we may go at the examination without necessarily deserving the reverse encomiums he bestowed on minute philosophers. He obviously intended the reader to set himself to work on them.

To say that Sterne was self-conscious is, I think, to say little. What he really seems to have wanted is self-consciousness from the reader.[1] It is a game, in short, that we play with the author. This game playing is, of course, a limitation to Sterne's art—not necessarily a fault. In the province of his own rhetoric, which plays with all affections of the middle range (those which, like those of *Don Quixote,* only hesitate with the sublime) to make them comment upon one another and reveal our motives—in this province he is unique. His own references to his rhetoric often define this province. I shall try to relate these references to larger motives of Sterne's strategy.

## 1. The Rhetoric of Existence

"Zounds!—————— Z——ds!" cried Phutatorius, deep in thought upon the dark regions within his breeches where Horror (a hot chestnut) had suddenly settled [4.26–30.318–331]. Tristram then circles the company, in conference concerning a possible flaw in the baptismal Latin already applied to himself with the disastrous name Tristram (rather than the propitious one, Trismegistus)—circles the table, drawing forth probable reasonings from each conferee for this "Z——ds!" (As always Tristram appears at once in at least two roles.) Among these inventions from effect to cause is one which supposes Phutatorius to have given the *"exordium"* to an oration, a reverse encomium on Yorick. (Any educated eighteenth-century reader would have known that Cicero and all his descendants had defined the exordium as a conciliation of the audience and a presaging of the manner of treatment.) On this knowledge, "Toby's good nature felt a pang for what Yorick was about to undergo." But this invention from "cause" is wrong, as it was certain to be, says Tristram, for though the inventions were proceeding from an "axiom" as good rhetorical enthymemes do,[2] the axiom was wrong, although very probable. "How finely we argue from mistaken facts!" says Tristram, and this may be taken as the true cause or state of his *rhetoric* which is so obviously in process in this story. (His paradoxical inventions on cause and effect by way of contrasts are the controlling form, in fact, of the *Life and Opinions.* They include antithetical characters who by their nature choose opinions which allow them the pleasure of settling into their own natures, that is, onto their Hobby-Horses; equivocations, many sexual, which proceed upon probable but vexed attitudes; and narratives, such as the Shandys' grand tour, which dramatize conflicting attitudes—all of which provide the rhetorical dynamic of dialectical question and answer in order to come at the arcane wells of the readers' affections.)

The rhetorical structure of this narrative of Phutatorius' hot chestnut is built upon an opening arraignment of Yorick by Didius, the Church lawyer and logician, for contempt of the conference. Calling up his logic, Didius attempts to hang Yorick upon the "two horns of my dilemma," a logical fallacy calculated for use by rhetoricians, with Aristotle's approval, as the figure "ceratin" or "horned argument." (Either the sermons are worthless or Yorick has committed sacrilege by his sarcasm.) Didius' horns are what anyone with proper indignation might say in deprecation of a parson who would tear up his sermons ostentatiously and distribute the pieces as pipe lights. But this rhetorical device permits Yorick (and Sterne) to expound his theory of sermons, which, in turn, the company reasons, has aggravated Phutatorius' latent dislike for Yorick and produced the "Z——ds!" as an exordium to a reverse encomium on the parson. But before he can go into the reasonings on the cause of Phutatorius' explosion, Sterne must, in the tradition of the facetious rhetor, be certain that the reader is engaged by a rhetorical gesture:

. . . a single word, and no more, uttered from the opposite side of the table, drew every one's ears towards it—a word of all others in the dictionary the last in that place to be expected—a word I am ashamed to write—yet must be written—must be read;—illegal—uncanonical—guess ten thousand guesses . . . —torture your invention for ever, you're where you was—In short, I'll tell it in the next chapter. [4.26.317–318]

To know what the word was, of course, the reader would have to know the cause of the interjection, which is the subject of equivocation by invention from cause for the next seven pages. So, with the reader's "invention" charged, Tristram proceeds to guide through a causal mystery which exhibits the very probable cross-workings of normal motives, a sort of dialectic through narrative. And even while vivifying through the most transfixing imagery Phutatorius' passion (namely, a newt on his privates), Sterne must remind the reader of the rhetoric under way; for his motive, as always, is not narrative, but *rhetorical description of an idea.* Phutatorius in a terrified disorder as the picture of a newt in his breeches utterly possesses his imagination utters the interjection thus, "Z——ds!—" and no more until the reasonings from all sides have well begun. This *"aposiopestick* break," says Tristram, was "as little as any man could have said upon the occasion;—and which . . . Phutatorius could no more help than he could the cause of it" [4.27.322]. It is not Phutatorius' "aposiopesis," in other words, but, rather, it belongs to the rhetoric of existence as men *will organize* existence to form conceptions. Existence makes a rhetorical figure of Phutatorius. Anyone hearing the "Z——ds!" would as a matter of course consider it an aposiopesis, presaging a proof of something. (As the artist, Sterne, of course, must take credit for this particular organization: "When great or unexpected events fall out upon the stage of this sublunary world—the mind of man . . . naturally takes a flight, behind the scenes, to see what is the cause and first spring of them—" [4.27.323].)

Phutatorius' mind finds the cause to be Yorick's attempt to make a living figure of allegoria out of him: " 'twas easily found out, that there was a mystical meaning in Yorick's prank—and that his chucking the hot chestnut into Phutatorius' ***-*****, was a sarcastical fling at his book—the doctrines of which, they said, had inflamed many an honest man in the same place. This *conceit* awaken'd Somnolentus—made Agelastes smile" [4.27.323]; however, as it turns out, it was a conceit not of Yorick's wit, but of Sterne's rhetoric, which, as each man speaks his piece, leads on to a burlesque of pedantry by way of St. Boniface's and Pope Zachary's findings on baptismal Latin—and ultimately to Sterne's espousal of common sense in matters legal, religious, and familiar, through Yorick's ironic and symbolic application of another rhetorical figure of fallacious logic, the *"argumentum commune"* to the whole discussion, which has now evolved to a scholastic proof that the child is no kin to its parents. This figure proposes what by quick statement can reinforce one side of an argument, but which by more careful examination is seen to do well for the other side. Given any vagary of existence, every man will create his own rhetoric.

The compass of this conference table is the compass of *Tristram Shandy*. Here are all the symbols and all the techniques, all the engines of rhetoric, which govern Shandy's "scurvy and disasterous world." Just outside the dialectic circle, though at the same time home, a baby in his crib, stands adult Tristram, measuring the natural dialogue of Affections by his rhetorical rules. Didius trots out his horned dilemma to hang up Yorick, who has ripped up a sermon with great show as the opening *figure,* a "sarcastick stroke," for his rhetoric about sermon-rhetoric. All because Fate (or Existence) has thrown in her own figure, a hot chestnut square into Phutatorius' breeches,—which he interprets as Yorick's sarcastic allegory. Naturally; for, after all, Phutatorius' own rhetoric has ever been directed toward inflaming the area where the chestnut has settled. His "Z——ds!" is taken by the company as exordium to an oration on Yorick, but Tristram uses it as an aposiopesis to engage the reader in this natural dialogue of the affections. Then the Church lawyers, base mechanicals, take over for their rhetorical show, a symbolic chorus to the whole proceedings. Meanwhile, Walter, the student of rhetoric, merely observes, and Toby puts in the *"argumentum fistulatorum"* ("Lillibullero"), *his* rhetoric. Yorick assumes his character of *eiron* by seeing the whole in the rhetorical frame of *"argumentum commune."* Every character, including Tristram and the reader, has assumed his natural rhetorical habit; each, *himself,* has become the figure of prosopopoeia, *just as in his sermons Sterne himself assumes different characters of prosopopoeia and conducts a dialogue.* This is Sterne's curious conduct of rhetoric; whereas it is ordinarily a discursive rather than intuitive art (as De Quincey points out), by Sterne's bringing rhetorical effects into consciousness by naming them, rhetoric becomes an intuitive, almost poetic, art, since the discursive quality becomes *not* an end in itself but a *symbol* of human communication.

We have seen how Sterne used Locke's theory of language as a form to exhibit Toby and Walter as *symbols* of the human communicative situation. The rhetorical forms work to the same end. Toby and Walter are in themselves a sort of rhetorical dialectic. In the middle of one of his lectures, during which Toby appears to be, but is not, "syllogizing" along with him, Walter must pull himself up short and drop his "metaphor" of "siege" in order to keep clear of Toby's fancy. And although Toby knows in his own heart that the true cause of long noses can be nothing but God, he is willing to whistle his rhetoric, "Lillibullero," with infinite benignity while Walter applies logic to the problem to find a true *cause* that will satisfy *him* [3.40–41.238–239]. Colonel Newcome is sometimes said to be a derivative of Uncle Toby. But there is no such rhetorical play between the good Colonel and his fellow characters; in fact, Thackeray himself cannot quite decide what to think of him, morally speaking. Sterne does not have that difficulty; Toby is one, but only one, statement of cause and effect. Give Toby and Walter the same cause and each will produce a characteristic, and therefore different, effect, each with his fraction of truth. Morally speaking, each is perfect, because each is a genuine, a real, question of existence. This is the way of rhetoric, the neutral art.

"Existence," in Sterne's world, seems almost personified, seems to state a topic, even give the exordium, and use the characters and reader as its factors to develop argument. Not doing, but expressing oneself, is the texture of life in this world. Toby, Walter, Slop, and the Shandy bull cannot ever quite do anything. Existence in the form of a hot chestnut, a sash window, or a squeaking parlor door provides the topic:

Every day for at least ten years together did my father resolve to have it mended . . . no family but ours would have borne with it an hour,—and what is most astonishing, there was not a subject in the world upon which my father was so eloquent, as upon that of door-hinges.—And yet at the same time, he was certainly one of the greatest bubbles to them, I think, that history can produce: his rhetoric and conduct were at perpetual handy-cuffs.
—Inconsistent soul that man is! . . . —his reason, that precious gift of God to him— . . . serving but to sharpen his sensibilities . . . [3.21.203].

Existence makes occasions, door hinges become symbols, and every man develops his characteristic rhetoric to establish his own being.

## 2. Rhetoric and Character

It is significant that every major character is placed in the situations described by Tristram in the terminology of classical rhetoric: Toby, in addition to his *argumentum fistulatorum,* twice becomes formally eloquent. Once when he first conceives the bowling-green war: "My

uncle Toby's eloquence brought tears into his [Walter's] eyes;—'twas
unexpected.—My uncle Toby, by nature, was not eloquent;—it had
the greater effect" [2.4.92]. He has lain in bed in suspended animation
for four years when the war is conceived. His eloquence, never known
before, results from his new need to persuade Walter of his character.
"A man and his Hobby-Horse . . . act and re-act exactly after the
same manner in which the soul and body do upon each other"
[1.24.77]. A man *is* his expression for Sterne. He can communicate
only by developing his own rhetoric. Thus Sterne reforms the old comic
idea of "humours": Shandean "humours" are not mere eccentricity,
but the very condition of communication in this world.

And later Toby delivers his "Apologetical Oration" on war
[6.32.459 ff.], which has all the rhetorical devices of Sterne's sermons.
(The formalities of rhetoric for Sterne are the natural symbols of the
formalities of ordinary communication; we are told that not one of the
characters of the book, not even Walter, has had rhetorical training.
Of course people do not really talk like rhetoricians in real life, but
*Tristram Shandy* is in no way naturalistic; it is in every regard a Cervantic association of the real abstract concerns of men with silly and
trifling events. And in every association there is a symbol of real life.
Rhetorical buffoonery, with all its silly conflicts and contrasts, is a
comic abstract of the real problem of communication.)

Walter, "born an orator," of course, is never unconscious of his
rhetorical situation, and the terminology of rhetoric is, we have seen,
the major language of his characterization.

Walter's natural gifts are displayed by showing him up before the
professors at Jesus College as not knowing the difference (out of books)
between *"ad hominem"* and *"ad ignorantium"* [1.19.52], but nevertheless on the preceding page he efficaciously defends his name theory
"in that soft and irresistible *piano* of voice, which the nature of *argumentum ad hominem* absolutely requires": "Your BILLY, Sir!—would
you, for the world, have called him JUDAS?" "I never knew a man able
to answer this argument," says Tristram, with real seriousness, for, in
truth, logic, paradoxical logic, *can* sharpen your sensibilities. As a
rhetorician, Walter indeed has a shrewd guess at the "weaknesses and
passions of his respondent." Thinking of his wife's refractory attitude
in the legal matter of childbirth, "set him upon running divisions upon

how many kinds of weaknesses there were . . . and then he would do
nothing but syllogize within himself" [1.16.42]. He packs up in his
rhetorical outfit all philosophies, and a library of illustrative narratives.
But he always says more than he knows. Sterne knows, however, and
uses Walter's rhetorical illustrations for the wider purpose of expressing
the controlling conceptions of the whole Shandean world in the discussion of the allegorical machinery of Slawkenbergius' Tale.* The tale,
before which all commentators seem to avert their eyes and have done
with a sibilant announcement that it contains something very vile,
illustrates Walter's thesis of noses; but, beyond Walter's comprehension, it illuminates Sterne's book. Thus one man's rhetoric becomes
both his character and a description of the world in which he finds
his being.

Trim also is a natural orator [5.6–7.359–361], particularly
strong in the category of Pronunciation, wondrous in "elocution"
[2.5.95]. His gestures are invincible:

> Ye who govern this mighty world and its mighty concerns with the *engines* of
> eloquence,—who heat it, and cool it, and melt it, and mollify it,—and then
> harden it again to *your purpose*—Ye who wind and turn the passions with this
> great windlass,—and, having done it, lead the owners of them, whither ye think
> meet—[a fair statement of Sterne's conception of rhetoric] . . . meditate—
> meditate, I beseech you, upon Trim's hat. [5.7.362]

His stance is recommended to all orators [2.17.122–123]. It will
be illustrated "in the parts of this cyclopaedia" where the instrumental
parts of eloquence fall under consideration. Slop too has a rhetorical
routine [3.15.186], but unfortunately he bungles it.† Finally, Mrs.
Shandy states her being by her silent, impervious eloquence in the marital bed "debates" which Walter has established as a regular occasion
for one Saturday and Sunday of each month [6.17–18.434–439].
Every character of the book, indeed, is primarily a rhetorical effect, a
device by which Tristram explicates his life *and opinions*.

## 3. Rhetoric, Knots, and Conceptualization

In each instance of their use, rhetorical processes and terms, *by being
named* or otherwise ostentatiously exhibited, function as symbols. The

---

*See above, chap. i, p. 18.
†See above, pp. 85, 86; below, pp. 116, 117.

snarling of one spring of conduct with another, by play between Sterne and the reader or among characters, is the only real source of dramatic energy in *Tristram*. The reader's rather ironic view of the whole field of this entanglement motive, even from the opening pages, prevents any large plot. Since time is change, the book has no time scheme, and therefore there is not even a development of the life situations of normal biography. Still, just as Sterne called his sermons "dramatic," he reminds the reader of *Tristram* that he is in the theater, and, indeed, upon the boards.* The snarls of conduct, the small tensions and irremediable knots which crossed affections assure, provide the entire action. There is never a new perspective; no new ground is reached from which to look back on the conflict past, as any respectable plot would provide. A knot cannot be undone without inspection of every turn of it, for *in the knot* is everything *Tristram* provides. *Symbolically,* Slop, the Romish goat, cannot even be allowed to cut the knot with which Obadiah has sealed his obstetrical kit, though his soul desperately cries to show off the mechanics of his accoucheurship. For, says Tristram, "In the case of these knots . . . and of the several obstructions, which, may it please your reverences, such knots cast in our way in getting through life—every hasty man can whip out his penknife and cut through them, —'Tis wrong" [3.10.168]. So Slop, pricked on by his pride in his mechanical infallibility, must sweat out his very ego in curses, which allows Walter the rhetorician the opportunity to trick him into reading Ernulphus' curse, a *reductio ad absurdum* of his own. In Ernulphus' curse are comprehended all the possible curses of this life, Tristram says. The dramatic scene becomes a complex conception of every man's need to curse.

Lest the reader doubt the rhetorical purpose of this particular tangle of characteristic expressions, Sterne punctuates it with a disquisition upon human nature and eloquence. He reminds us first that our rules of propriety in oaths as in other fields of expression, in painting, acting, or writing, are only the desiccated remains of the copious "invention" [3.12–14.180–186] of freer spirits (such as Ernulphus) who were not befetished with the cant of criticism. Raphael did not strive for the grace of Raphael, nor did Titian imitate the coloring of Titian. True genius has its own copia of invention. Next, Slop, recovering himself,

---

*See chap. vii, below.

thinks to triumph yet over Walter for his slight in putting him under the command of the midwife upstairs. Slipping into Toby's military metaphor, he proceeds to a rhetorical argument, "a singular stroke of eloquence (at least it was so, when eloquence flourished at Athens and Rome, and would be so now, did orators wear mantles)" [3.14.185]. As ancient orators after building to a climax of mystery or intensity discovered from their mantles "a scar, an axe, a sword, a pink'd-doublet, a rusty helmet, a pound and a half of pot-ashes in an urn, or a three-halfpenny pickle pot,—but above all, a tender infant royally accoutred," to complete the meaning of a suddenly ruptured discourse, so Slop with military metaphor prepares a climax at which he intends to pull his homemade forceps from the at last undone satchel. Alas, Obadiah has jumbled things so badly that Slop's fumbling takes off the oratorical effect and Toby's "argument" prevails. In the tangles of this rhetorical knot the causes and effects of three personalities, Toby's, Walter's, and Slop's, have been displayed, with a measure of good sense from each. Even Slop has some truth to tell; *all three* have *all* the truth in this particular situation to tell. In short, they are figures of prosopopoeia in a rhetorical proof.

Knots *are* important in this book. They are conceptions. There is one curious convolution of Toby and Walter that appears to have been imported to *Tristram Shandy* directly from a divine oration of the "lousy prebendary" of York Cathedral [4.6–7.276–278]. Walter's last philosophical hope has just been overthrown by Dr. Slop's forceps, which have crunched the new Tristram's nose, when, shifting his attitude (he has fallen flat across the bed, a grand gesture of an orator, except that in this case, unfortunately, one despairing hand has dropped into the chamber pot, necessitating an adjustment of attitude), Walter begins an oration to Toby. "Attitudes are nothing, madam,—'tis the transition from one attitude to another—like the preparation and resolution of a discord into harmony, which is all in all." The transition from one attitude to another happens to be the pervading strategy of Sterne's Shandean sermons, and, as it happens, Walter's address once *was* a sermon ("Trust in God"), and in the sermon "Walter" and "Toby" are conflicting ideas which are used as a sort of dialectic to come at the final point: our ego must fail us in the end if there is not a religious trust in God. And, in the sermon, like Walter, the auditor is pictured "upon a bed of languishing": what is it that finally makes us bear the evils we experience? Is it that secret spring of ego, self-love, which forces us to hope for better (Walter)? Or is it merely the favor of God (Toby)? " . . . 'tis wonderful by what hidden resources the mind is enabled to stand it out, and bear itself up, as it does against the impositions laid upon our nature," says Walter. " 'Tis by the assistance of Almighty God," cries Toby. "That is cutting the knot, said my father, instead of untying it.—But give me leave to lead you, brother Toby, a little deeper into this mystery." Walter thereupon changes his attitude to that of Socrates in the painting by Raphael, in which the ancient master of dialectic "holds the fore-finger of his left hand between the fore-finger and the thumb of his right, and seems as if he was saying . . . '*You grant me* this—and this: and this, and this, I don't ask of you—they follow of themselves in course'." Here by his references to rhetoric Sterne gives a clear exposition of his own method. Frequently the characters of *Tristram* are really prosopopoeia, personifications of attitudes which are set at each other in dialectic form, question and answer, statement and equivocation upon statement. In the sermon from which this passage was taken for *Tristram Shandy,* Walter and Toby are attitudes by the opposition of which the preacher develops his dramatic rhetoric. In *Tristram* they make *one* conception.

## 4. An Ethical Proof: The Man of Humor

Pointing out to the critics that there are at least six "places" for their arguments against him (in the metaphor of dining-table places, but punning on the "places" of rhetorical argument),[3] Tristram develops one in particular, the contradiction he has made in the character of Uncle Toby by making him both a military man of acumen and such a "confused, pudding-headed, muddle-headed fellow, as—Go look."

"So, Sir Critick, I could have replied; but I scorn it.—'Tis language unurbane,—and only befitting the man who cannot . . . dive deep enough into the first causes of human ignorance . . ." Besides, says Tristram, such a reply would be no better argument than Toby's "Lilli-bullero," and he as an author is a man of erudition, with "similes," "metaphors," "allusions," "illustrations," and "must sustain my character properly, and contrast it properly too." And so with this ethical proof (from the character of the speaker) he proceeds to Locke to get at the causal arcana in Toby's behavior. [2.2.85.]

Like Yorick, Sterne found it necessary to post pasquinades along his way, and as in Yorick's case they were not lost for want of gathering. His reputation as a "foul satyr" (Thackeray's encomium) has fallen off recently, but he would, I think, have been less concerned about the extravagance of the opinion than about the disinclination of his readers to see his first-person character as a reverse ethical proof of a perverse rhetoric. Whether Sterne was or was not Shandy is in one way not beside the point. In reality he was not merely Tristram, but all the Shandys, with Slop, Yorick, and other ingredients. In short, he was a rhetorician using his characters and their "humours" as devices of rhetoric.

If the reader is willing to see Tristram (and Sterne) not merely as a buffoon, but as a clown whose roles dramatize his insights, he has gone a long way toward understanding the Shandean world. This essential difference is exactly defined as the difference between a Humourist and a Man of Humour, by Corbyn Morris in his contemporary (1744) *Essay towards fixing the true standards of Wit, Humour, Raillery, Satire and Ridicule:*

> It may be also proper to describe a Man of Humour, and an Humourist, which are very different persons.
> A Man of Humour is one, who can happily exhibit a weak and ridiculous Character in real Life, either by assuming it himself, or representing another in it, so naturally, that the whimsical Oddities and Foibles, of that character, shall be palpably expos'd.
> Whereas an Humorist is a Person in real Life, obstinately attached to sensible peculiar Oddities of his own genuine Growth, which appear in his Temper and Conduct.
> In short, a Man of Humour is one, who can happily exhibit and expose the Oddities and Foibles of an Humourist, or of other Characters.

That rhetoric always potentially is a game—when rhetoric becomes the topic, necessarily a game—Sterne's constant references to his own rhetorical effects, very often in the nomenclature of the classical manuals, remind the reader. The techniques by which the reader is implicated, in his own character, in the proofs of satirical rhetoric, is forced to assume the double attitude of superiority on the one hand and involvement on the other, are the constant study of the satirist. The *ingénu* narrator and the related device, the foolish narrator, like

Erasmus' Folly protesting ineptitude, blundering upon obfuscated relations between sanity and insanity, vulgarity and refinement, heroics and
mean rascality, are mechanisms by which the reader is involved.
Tristram's foolish, shifting character, his appearance now as a buffoon,
now as a strangely perceptive observer of "humours," now as a series
of voices in argument, now as a vile equivocator — as the Man of
Humour—working his persuasion is of course one method of forcing
the reader to participate in argument. He adds to this game the hyperbolic development of the traditional figures of communication with the
reader: rhetorical question, anticipation, doubting and deliberation,
digression, mock logic, logical reduction to absurdity, equivocation,
meiosis (a sort of reverse climax), and ellipsis. And the effects of ironic
distance are achieved very often simply by *naming* or otherwise ostentatiously exhibiting the devices for involving the reader. We see that
we are supposed to take part with the author in the consideration of the
ways in which we are influenced. Our own stated consciousness becomes
a primary material of the meaning. This cannot be so in pure narrative
or in a serious rhetoric. A forensic orator, for example, would probably
not ask the jury to consider his last, most subtle device. Tristram's
devices keep the reader *in* the narrative, make him an actor on the stage.

But though Sterne's style depends so largely upon figures and devices
of communication, with argumentation as a way to *a* conclusion, we
have seen, he gets nowhere. Unlike a later dialectician, Shaw, he had
few axes to grind. Even his sermons, which presumably would have
Christian doctrine to prove by pathetic or logical argument, seem
blunted in their conclusions. "The Prodigal Son," for example, by every
figure of communication plays upon the audience's affections and attitudes, and yet the logical conclusion is so vapid that Sterne tacked on
a silly, fatuous (not intended so this time) disquisition on the grand tour
to make all his argumentation apply to something statable. The forms
of argument for Sterne but state the complications in the argument. It
was the *process* of argument, not the argument itself, that interested
Sterne, for in the process minds describe themselves.

Fundamentally the argumentative forms of Tristram *are* symbols.
In themselves usually too silly to bear any serious polemical weight,
they become symbols of the inevitable and necessary (for total conception) conflict of personal organizations of phenomena, and by naming

and otherwise directing attention to his forms Sterne has made them serve also to shift the reader's focus from subjective to objective perception.

It is quite clear, for example, that the exordium, as it were, to the rhetoric of Slawkenbergius is Tristram's long (and I am afraid, tiresome) equivocation on the "definition" of nose: ". . . heaven is witness, how the world has revenged itself upon me for leaving so many openings to equivocal strictures" [3.31.218]. Then he gives the reader the tautological "definition," "by the word *Nose* . . . I mean a Nose, and nothing more, or less." With thus an allusion to Locke's philosophical stricture on definition, Tristram proceeds to the rhetorical technique of inventing from the "place" of "definition" a complex meaning. As it agitates the slumbers of the Strassburg nuns and ruptures the citizens' quiet, so Slawkenbergius' nose is intended to intrude itself into the reader's fancy.

Definition (and division of definitions) is one of Sterne's characteristic devices of invention. In his long burlesque of that eighteenth-century cliché, "wit and judgment," in the "Author's Preface" [3.20.192–203], he assumes different roles in an elaborate mock "dialectic induction" to prove the possibilities of this cliché in the world: one's "invention" (faculty which finds arguments) need only be turned to a consideration of the different affections which hide their identity in such trite formulas. By shifting his ground, the artist can define the compound motives hidden in even a cliché. The whole rhetorical invention on love and Uncle Toby's confusion therein hinges on Tristram's initial equivocation: " . . . Are you to imagine . . . that I shall set out [in the system of love] with a description of *what love is?*" [6.36.466]. Again, later, this frustration of the reader's right to a definition is turned to the work at hand: love is bound to confuse when it means "hatred," "sentiment," "nonsense," and so on [8.4.542]. Further on, Tristram offers a Rabelaisian alphabetical definition of love [8.13.551].

Tristram makes clear the necessary perversity of his rhetoric by immediately quoting thereupon from Walter, the master of oratory. " 'You can scarce,' said he, 'combine two ideas upon it, brother Toby, without an hypallage'." The way to define, says Locke, is to combine ideas; but, says Tristram the rhetorician (through Walter), you can scarce combine without a "hypallage." Since hypallage is syntactical interchange which imputes to one subject the attributes of another, in effect Tristram asks what is subject and what is accident in love. The difficulties of definition are obvious. Puttenham[4] defines hypallage: "A certain piteous lover, to move his mistress to compassion, wrote among other amorous verses, this one: Madame, I set your eyes before mine woes." Sterne's mention of the term is in a sense poetic, for it serves as a symbol of the difficulty of living (in this case, loving) by definitions.

Merely the naming of a metaphor can also produce that standard device of Sterne's style, the sudden shifting of attitude, effecting an ironical aesthetic distance from the matter at hand which reforms its meaning. Six times, at least, Tristram announces elaborately that he must "drop" a metaphor, thus making one attitude comment upon another. Speaking of Toby's mistaking of the word "bridge" as it was spoken (in regard to Tristram's nose) for a literal military object, Tristram comments that he must give an exact account of the "road" that led to it "or to drop my metaphor, (for there is nothing more dishonest in an historian, than the use of one,)—in order to conceive the probability of this error in my uncle Toby aright, I must give you some account of an adventure of Trim's, though much against my will . . ." [2.23.206–207]. With Toby on the "road" we see a wire-drawn simpleton marching as he is maneuvered by a mad association of ideas, but, the metaphor dropped, we get into a very real and sentimental story. Sterne means us to keep both attitudes toward Toby. Sterne's metaphors often thus are not allowed to serve in their *own significations;* rather they are pointed out as part of the thinking process of human beings and are therefore a symbol *only of that thinking process.* This is the usual effect that Sterne achieves in making rhetoric the subject of rhetoric.

Similarly apostrophe, along with other exclamatory figures, is comic bombast but also a sort of punctuation, a mark where the reader is to change attitudes from sympathetic participation in a theme to an ironic and conceptual detachment from it. After all, in serious usage apostrophe is prescribed as a device of the sublime or high style. (The flickering end of Le Fever over which nineteenth-century critics wept and raged and at which Tristram smiles in mocking himself is just another example of his perception of the tenuous pathetic-bathetic quality of hyperbolic effects. This is part of his meaning.) For Tristram's outbreaks are platform technique (there are at least a dozen notices to the reader of the theatrical nature of the book), and often they serve to isolate narrative sequences as illustrations of the arguments at hand.

These figures that so affect tone — apostrophe and invocation, aposiopesis, and digression—are pointed out many times. Aposiopesis, like apostrophe, is properly a figure of the sublime, indicating great commotion in the speaker's breast. In Tristram it is usually a device of a festive irony. Irony, not ridicule. It is not a device to denote absurdity, as it could be by a simple inversion of the sublime. Phutatorius' "aposiopestick break," and Slop's, too, make their emotions real, but at the same time detach the reader. We know too much about the passions of both characters to consider them as mere satiric figures. There is a measure of real pathos in both, as expressed by their aposiopeses, but at the same time the element of Cervantic sublimity makes an ironic tone predominant.

So with Toby's aposiopesis [2.6.100]: "My sister, I dare say, added he, does not care to let a man come so near her ****. I will not say whether my uncle Toby had completed the sentence or not;—'tis for his advantage to suppose he had . . . If, on the contrary, my uncle Toby had not fully arrived at his period's end,—then the world stands indebted to the snapping of my father's tobacco-pipe, for one of the neatest examples of that ornamental figure in oratory, which Rhetoricians stile the *Aposiopesis.*" Here follows a dissertation on the right end (i.e., purpose) of a woman. Certain definite questions arise. Did Toby use the figure at all, for maybe he had said all he intended? Here, we see Walter as a man who must himself create occasions for his orations and who like every male relishes the opportunity to speculate on the right end of a woman. Or perhaps Toby is really befuddled about females. This is one of the big problems of Toby's life, comical to the reader but not entirely so since Toby is an entirely sympathetic character and sympathy makes the sexual implications rather compelling. Or, finally, perhaps this is just more of Tristram's vile bawdy, by which he gives pain, as Coleridge said, to innocent modesty. In any case, the only possible attitude for the reader who is playing the game is irony. The figure "aposiopesis" *in itself, in its ordinary rhetorical use,* has no function. As a device of tone, it becomes a symbol of the ironic view of the mundane concerns of life.

So Sterne's devices of syntax are *devices,* quite consciously wrought, and not vagaries of a sensible mind, associating according to an occult logic. The whole meaning of his discussion of time, we have seen, depends upon the reader's holding the fractured syntax of one sentence (Toby's as he starts to ring the bell) in mind while a forty-page digression explores the character of the speaker.* The burlesque of Locke on time would not be accomplished without this precise break in the syntax. If the reader does not see it as a conscious device, if he assumes the break to be whimsy, the whole effect and meaning is lost. Similarly, the structures of the less spectacularly tenuous sentences, those accomplished in a line or a dozen lines, are not mere funny typographics. The typographical antics, indeed, are only another of Sterne's wry signals to the reader by which he points out rhetorical devices as symbols of thought processes. Swift was able to turn the extravagant pseudo-Elizabethan Grub Street jargon, so reminiscent of Thomas Nashe's style, to his own peculiar satiric ends in *A Tale of a Tub*. Swift knew the indecorous stylistic of the Tom Browns and used it to play the fool. The fool is a device, and though *A Tale of a Tub* recommends the supreme happiness of the state of being a fool among knaves, we know that Swift himself was not a fool among knaves. The entirely different style of *Gulliver* is again a fool's device; it is like the plain style of Dryden, but of course it is not plain, for all is a vast trope of irony. Similarly Sterne's indecorous style is a conscious device, a *professional* fool at work. (Shandy is possibly Yorks cant for buffoon.) Other professional literary fools such as Swift and Erasmus (whose Folly also uses hyperbolic rhetorical lingo) had other, steadier faces; Sterne played the role all the way, and asks for recognition of the role as a device only by his continual notice of his own stylistic tricks. Enough has already been said to show that his forte was not whimsy, but a studied, relentless burlesque of rhetorical techniques by which he writes a history of the mind in terms of constantly conflicting attitudes. His indecorous use of the traditional syntactical devices of asyndeton (series unconnected by coördinate conjunctions), or division of a subject into its parts or from its antecedents, of the Rabelaisian catalogue, of turn and antithesis, of parenthesis and digression, of zeugma, and of anticlimax—his constant hyperbolic use of these devices, supports always the war of attitudes. Trim, of course, orates "without antithesis or point or turn," while

---

*See above, chap. ii, pp. 36–42.

Walter "proceeds from period to period by metaphor and allusion," but both, together with the rest of the *dramatis personae,* function as voices in the war of attitudes. And in his own voice Tristram shifts his style as often as his characters and narrative. Volume 7, for example, is a dissertation on how to run before Death, the burden of which is that Death catches those whose sensibilities, intellectuals, and feet stand still. The mazy syntax is part of the burden. The book opens in the middle of a conversation with the reader, a conversation which never had a beginning, then a dash, correction of the reader's assumption that *Tristram* and its author are interminable. Dash. A cough and tetchy spirits, body and soul, are to be contended with. They are terminals. End paragraph, new consideration of the spirits. Eulogy of the spirits, parenthesis, but they have made me a fool, colon, the use of the spirits, series of phrases, they have made the ways of the world neither sable nor sickly green, have given hope, and when Death . . . , end series. Dash. Death speaks. New situation, a lewd joke is in progress with Eugenius. Dash. Death speaks. Eugenius speaks and shows by his speech that Death has gone, doubting his commission, having met such blithe spirits. Then dash. Tristram speaks. The jig is up, though, the son of a whore has found out his lodging. Dash. Eugenius speaks. Whore— sin. Dash. Tristram speaks. But, sinner or no, one must get his life lived. Series of phrases developing this theme. The body is sin but also has two legs and can run through the world as well as dance with Death. I'll gallop across Europe to the *world's end* and pray God that he [Death] may break his neck. The syntax, too, in a series of dashed phrases gallops to "world's end." Dash. Pun on "world's end," Eugenius speaking now. "He runs more risk *there,* said Eugenius, than thou." The pun exactly defines the conceptual range of the whole passage, the range from the body to the spirit. And so the passage ends with wit, sentiment, pleasure, sensuality, art, life and death, and God, slapdash heaped in a *necessary* confusion. Necessary because of the human situation. This is *not* free association; the terms, the voices are united in one conception. But it is the fractured, hyphenated style that demonstrates the impossibility of merely literal meaning; for by means of the very extravagant, foolish syntax attitudes shift and redefine one another and imitate the fabric of living that can be seen only through a fool's eyes. Only a fool would put English words together with such indecorum. Only a foolish reader would fail to understand that the very extravagance of the syntax is one more method by which Sterne calls the reader to self-consciousness, and to notice of his author's self-consciousness.

The skein continues to tangle. A chapter of Rabelaisian expletives, puns, and unannounced voices. No conjunctions, only dashes. Another fractured exploration of the subject, How to run before Death. Is this, the reader *must* ask, a travel story, or are we who are only readers to be forced to stand puzzling over the same evolving ideas, never holding any in a clear light or the same light? The answer is a threat to offer up real travel literature: fifty pages of Rapin's minute but romantic account of the seige of Calais.

With this unnerving threat the chapter ends. This is not respectable literature, and the proper reader is reminded of the impropriety at the beginning of the next chapter, where the author kindly abjures his power (all the while reinforcing it): "But courage! gentle reader!—I scorn it—'tis enough to have thee in my power—" [7.6.486].

Thus, again, he draws the reader's attention to his last most subtle device. The indecorous syntax and mad typography, as other devices, can demonstrate the history of the mind.

Later, Tristram sees himself as an act. "O England! England! . . . cried I, kneeling upon one knee, as I was beginning my apostrophe—" [7.34.562–527]. He is observing himself an English traveler put upon by French trumpery. He makes a pun on the French water-transportation tax after a French official catches him on one knee and asks if he is in want of the aids of the Church. "I go by WATER—said I—and there's another will be for making me pay for going by oyl [i.e., extreme unction]." When we remember that the trip is for the sole purpose of fleeing before that son of a whore, Death, the rhetorical bombast of apostrophe and pun becomes a serious symbolic irony as well as a jest. The whole narrative becomes an illustration of an idea. This sudden isolation of an idea is often accomplished by the tonal devices of exclamation; it reinforces the sudden shifts in thought which the criss-crossed questionings produce.

As for "digression," though it is a standard figure of classical rhetoric,[5] intended to conciliate or confuse the audience, in Sterne's use it is simply another device of contrast. And contrast certainly is the pervading form of the book. Yet there is nothing adventitious in Tristram's digressions: they conciliate (often negatively) and confuse, certainly, but, more important, they advance the rhetorical motives. They do so because Sterne's purpose is not to come to a logical denouement, but to describe the mental workings of either the characters or the reader. In this process a digression is analogous in its effect to the other devices of contrast—communication with the reader in different characters, division and complication of causes, sudden shifts in tone, syntax, and so on, the devices already discussed above and treated in the following chapter as elements of the dramatic structure of the book. A digression is one way by which a problem is explored and in the end resolved, not in a logical proof, but in a *conception* of the whole.

This digressive principle is Sterne's distinct achievement, "executed in a masterly kind of fashion," as he tells us, "the merit of which has all along, I fear, been overlooked by my reader." How, indeed, does the reader think he has developed character? "By this contrivance [digression] the machinery of my work is of a species by itself; two contrary motions are introduced into it, and reconciled, which were thought to be at variance with each other" [1.22.72–73]. Any character, any conception in *Tristram Shandy* is developed by obvious contrasts. As has already been suggested above, the unity of the book is preserved by dramatic irony: from the outset in Volume I the reader knows the entire scope of action, and the digressions are therefore not useful for the purposes of plot, but for reinforcing the ironic conception. By digressions within digressions for example, Tristram can be in three places at once [7.18.516]: "I am this moment walking across the market-place of Auxerre . . . and I am this moment also entering Lyons . . . and I am moreover this moment . . . upon the banks of the Garonne, . . . where I now sit rhapsodizing all these affairs." The crossing of affections is accomplished by digressions, among other devices, but by making his reader take note at various points of the digression mechanism, Sterne practically pleads for an ironical attitude toward the events of his work—and yet he is accused of an uncritical, sentimental self-indulgence!

A final figure which we might consider, since Tristram so often reminds the reader of his most subtle rhetorical effects gained by its use, is "equivocation." We can never forget the "openings to equivocal strictures," and Tristram encourages us to do our worst. But as it always turns out, the worst we can do is reveal our own participation in certain ideas, some pornographical. But enough has already been said of Sterne's equivoques, on nose, on whiskers, on Slawkenbergius' Tale, on Toby's aposiopesis, on Phutatorius' hot chestnut, on Tristram's conception, and so on, to permit a conclusive statement without further demonstration. The equivoques (sometimes, admittedly, silly in a way Sterne did not intend) always bring out certain definite attitudes or affections, and these definite attitudes are always in conflict. Here is but one more device in Sterne's history of the mind, in which he makes the reader's mind, with the reader's aid, the laboratory of his demonstration.

These interpretations of Sterne's purpose in bringing his own rhetorical devices to the reader's notice throughout the book are intended to show his use of traditional forms for original motives, the use of forms as symbols of the thinking process, and also to examine the "self-consciousness" which nearly every critic remarks in *Tristram Shandy*. In sum the "self-consciousness" seems actually to be a *device* to involve the reader in the arguments of the book and at the same time to give him the detachment necessary to dramatic irony. For by tying his knots of argument and feeling, and then by pointing to the devices of his rhetoric, Sterne asks the reader to examine the ways of thought and feeling and to see them not as peculiar to individual characters, but as symbolic of various aspects of Everyman's, including the reader's, mind.

# CHAPTER SEVEN · *Rhetorical Structure as Drama*

## 1. Dramatic
## Development
THE PREACHER Sterne, after at last getting the Prodigal Son home from his Oriental grand tour, fleeced but restored to filial piety, breaks out his culminating apostrophe, "O ye affections! How fondly do you play at cross-purposes with each other." This sermon, as we have seen, is in substance nothing but the affections at cross purposes, not only of the Biblical characters but also of the reader or auditor. " 'Tis the natural dialogue of true transport," we are told; and truly it is, for, on the single vehicle of crossed affections, the Prodigal has been conveyed through Persia, Damascus, Babylon, India, and Egypt. This natural dialogue, brought to a more earthy arena, informed by a radical perception and whole conception, is the only continuity of Sterne's drama in *Tristram Shandy*. His invention was not fragmentary; it discovers, from first word to last, an integral association of ideas—never casual, nor intended to simulate the unconscious—that evokes a precise world of conception. The book is of a piece. As continuously reiterative as, we have seen, are the *forms* of Sterne's inventions, the associations themselves have a continuous and

129

inevitable development until the last volume, the proper denouement, when Mrs. Wadman's venereal eye is deflowered, Toby makes an association of ideas between HUMANITY and lust, and Walter's last hypothesis is battered to pieces by an impotent bull, a very type of the Shandys. The world is all behind us, all made up. Whether the book was finished or not is an easy question, therefore, to answer. Sterne was a man of taste and he had said precisely enough on the topics he had presented to his invention. New topics, by an act of the will, obviously might have served to continue the book, but what better punctuation than the bull (apparently one that "might have done for Europa herself in purer times") now found out a mock hero. "L———d! said my mother, what is all this story about?" The dramatic structure of the book is a dialogue of the affections that has both movement and ultimate completion.

The many references to drama throughout *Tristram Shandy* show that Sterne thought of the book as a drama and of the drama as a developing play of ideas and affections at cross purposes. And the references to drama perform precisely as do those to rhetoric: they serve to involve the reader's sensibilities in the artist's perception of the form by which the human mind is affected. They preserve the reader's sense of irony. Consider, for example, the following scene: Tristram's nose has been crushed and Walter has decided upon the name Trismegistus to undo the mischief. With Toby he starts down the stairs [4.9.279], launching on the first step a dissertation on Chance, for though he has just finished a disputation (taken from Sterne's sermon)[1] on the secret spring (hope founded in the ego) within us which counterbalances the evils of life, and though his new hope is the name of Trismegistus, he realizes, he says, that Chance is indisputable. Toby says he knows nothing of Chance, and while saying it he accidentally strikes Walter a terrible blow on the shin with his crutch. The dialectic of living, one event answering, defining another, has proved Walter's thesis about Chance, and this pleasure takes off the agony on his shinbone. With Toby and Walter only halfway down the stairs, and with their affections at complete odds, Tristram fixes them on the landing for a chapter of his own discourse, the only topic of which is his own rhetoric. The irony of the narrative is already obvious: Tristram-to-be is never going to be Trismegistus, we know, and to supplement this piece of dramatic irony Tristram must remind us that the crossed affections between Toby and

Walter, exhibited stair by stair, are of the essence of the *book's* drama:
"Is it not a shame to make two chapters of what passed in going down
one pair of stairs? for we are got no farther yet than to the first landing,
and there are fifteen more steps down to the bottom; and for aught I
know, as my father and my uncle Toby are in a talking humour, there
may be as many chapters as steps;— . . . Sir, I can no more help it
than my destiny:—A sudden impulse comes across me—*drop the curtain,* Shandy . . ." [4.10.281; italics mine.]

   This is the chapter upon chapters, in which we are informed that "in
a work of this dramatic cast they are as necessary as the shifting of
scenes." Whatever can set the conflict of affections in relief so that it
asks a new, complicating question is useful to Sterne as a rhetorical
device. The little stair scene is a demonstration of one of the main points
of the book: the fact that many of Walter's abstract theses would be as
respectable as Montaigne's (an influence acknowledged by Sterne), and
of the same sort, had they not reference to such concrete absurdities and
were they not run down into absolute systems;—and this fact merely
adds one more dramatic conflict of the affections: the human propensity
for seeing every silly and trifling event as a symbol of some great theoretical concern. Walter is in himself one aspect of Everyman's mind.

   We proceed down the stairs. Susannah goes bounding by, with a
snippy answer for her master's inquiry about the welfare of the baby.
Then we are in the middle of another dialectical investigation on the
cause of human affections. Of all the riddles of married life, says Walter,
none has more intricacies in it than this, "that from the very moment the
mistress of the house is brought to bed, every female in it, from my
lady's gentlewoman down to the cinder-wench, becomes an inch taller
for it; and give themselves more airs upon that single inch, than all their
other inches put together" [4.12.284]. But Toby, all humanity, thinks
it is because men then feel an inch smaller: " 'Tis a piteous burden upon
'em, continued he, shaking his head." "Yes, yes, 'tis a painful thing,"
Walter replies, shaking *his* head. But "never did two heads shake
together, in concert, from two such different springs."

   "God bless ⎫ 'em all," said Toby.
   "Duce take ⎭            said Walter.

   Tristram has just told us that this is drama, and the printer's brace
that grips the opposite statements is an emblem of his idea of drama.

The brace itself is a device he uses occasionally throughout the book to symbolize crossed ideas or affections. The emblematic stairs and its burden of the dialogue of Chance and Hope and Birth and Women and Sympathy and Reason has a necessary connection to every event in the first four volumes and leads to every one of the next five. Each topic ultimately finds complete conceptualization. There *is* real development in this history of the mind.

At least in another dozen places in the book, Tristram sets off various rhetorical effects by pointing to their dramatic quality. It has been argued in this discussion that the characters are a sort of prosopopoeia (personification of a dialectical voice) by which the narrator discourses, a heightening of the technique of the sermons, the preacher, in order to set varying emotions at odds, assuming various characters in a dialogue argument. Nothing makes clearer Sterne's dramatic sense than the beginning of the long series of inventions* on the topic of love in the story of Toby and the Widow. When Toby's hobby-horse is broken down by the Treaty of Utrecht, Tristram comes on stage to ask the reader's services as stagehand: "I beg the reader will assist me here, to wheel my uncle Toby's ordnance behind the scenes . . . and clear the theatre . . . ;—that done, my dear friend Garrick, we'll snuff the candles bright . . . and exhibit my uncle Toby dressed in a new character" [6.29.455]. But before the puppets are recostumed, Toby, allowed to be intimate and human for another moment, must make, in Ciceronian style, an "apologetical oration" for war, with figures of communication, apostrophe, prosopopoeia, repetition of sentence elements, parallelism and antithesis, and, in conclusion, a brilliant sententia. Toby, we remember, never thought of a rhetorical figure in his life, but every character of *Tristram Shandy* orates formally when he finds a compelling need to express his soul. By rhetorical formulas Sterne represents the human communicative situation in which every communicant perforce must achieve his own rhetoric, must find the available means of persuasion and express himself in formulas that naturally engage the affections. Form, then, for Sterne is a necessity of *nature*. This aspect of Toby orated away, there begins the complete system of love [6.36.466]. Drama here is the mental action developed by continuously shifting forms.

---

*Discussed as rhetorical structure on pp. 140 ff., below.

In another scene [2.18.143] Tristram has just begun to lay the intimate details of the three-cornered debate between Walter, Toby, and Slop on the proper attitude toward women in labor (expressed subsequently by each in his own rhetoric), when Tristram breaks off Toby's sentence and begins to discourse about his drama: "I have dropp'd the curtain over this scene for a minute,—to remind you of one thing,—and to inform you of another" [2.19.144]. From the intimacy of the stage we are jerked to the foyer for a conference with the author; from interest in the narrative for its own sake, we are jerked into an interest in the narrative as symbol.

All this is Sterne's meaning for drama. Not just conflict, then, but development of conceptions by a creative association of ideas is of its essence. One form, one event, one affection, ironically isolating and redefining another, in turn asking a new question: this is the dynamic principle of Sterne's drama. For the true feeler of humor, he wrote, " 'tis like reading *himself* and not the *book*." By the last volume, all the topics of rhetorical development which have been discussed are completely circumscribed and yet interrelated. But precisely because it is part of rhetoric, Sterne could never write drama for the theater. There is too much of the rhetorician involved; no narrative exists for itself, but all is in illustration of the narrator's proposition. The "I" is so intimately bound up in the action of the book that it is impossible to imagine how the events would come off without the narrator's connections. Toby and Walter could not argue on a legitimate stage, because every argument depends upon some general statement about human nature which Tristram must deliver. Every vignette is dependent upon the narrator's rhetorical purpose. In truth, Sterne as the rhetorical preacher could never get himself out of his stories long enough to make them subsist in themselves as plotted structures. Had he been less the rhetorician, he might have been more the dramatist. The only possible way to imagine *Tristram Shandy* as a play is to imagine Tristram in front of the curtain as a chorus or commentator pointing to the stage action; and then the sense of freedom, of the voices as a simple dialectic of nature, would be lost. The drama is one of ideas, not actions. In writing to Garrick, whom he sought out first in London for a friend, Sterne made his stagestruck state clear: "I sometimes think of a Cervantic comedy upon these and the materials of the third and fourth volumes which will be still more dramatick,—tho I as often distrust its success, unless at the Universities. Half a word of encouragement would be enough to make me conceive, and bring forth something for the stage (how good, or how bad, is another story)."[2] Curtis, in his note for this letter, quotes from the memoirs of a contemporary: " . . . once meeting him [Sterne] at Drury-lane Theatre, I said to him, 'As you are so intimate with Garrick, I wonder that you have never undertaken to write a comedy.' He seemed quite struck, and after a pause, with tears in his eyes, replied, 'I fear I do not possess the proper talent for it . . .' " He did not have the proper talent because he had himself (in some mask) to be present in every action. His peculiar rhetoric made the dramatic quality of *Tristram* but prevented its becoming drama.

## 2. *Two Views of the Rhetorical Structure*

In the following analysis, from Volume I, chap. i *et seqq.*, an attempt is made to take the guides to his invention which I have discussed and trace in a developing dramatic sequence the concerns not of Tristram, Yorick, Walter, or Toby, but of the reader—to trace Sterne's history of the mind. The material of the analysis is that of the opening pages of *Tristram* because it is here that the transition from the pulpit orator to the facetious rhetor is most obvious. In the first part of the volume Sterne assiduously made his moral reflections after weaving each knot of the affections, but as the volume progressed his rhetoric became more implicit, and, though the same methods for crossing affections appear, the reflection upon them is not so often stated. After the analysis of the volume's opening explicit rhetoric, we may then turn to the implicit variety following, where we shall see the same motives and ideas find final development.

In the opening sentence of *Tristram* the reader enters the fomenting stream of equivocation, a stream which at one point is apostrophized: "impetuous fluid! the moment thou pressest against the flood-gates of the brain—see how they give way!—in swims Curiosity, beckoning to her damsels to follow—they dive into the center of the current—Fancy sits musing upon the bank . . . —and Desire, with vest held up to the knee . . . snatches at them as they swim by . . ." "I wish," says Tristram, in starting his story. No fact is offered for the reader's orientation, only the figure "optatio" or "wish," a figure impossible to resist and so calculated to open the auditor's mind. Further on [3.1.157], Toby, about to declaim from his Hobby-Horse, bemuses Slop with the same device: "My uncle Toby's wish did Dr. Slop a disservice which his heart never intended any man,—Sir, it confounded him— . . . thereby putting his ideas into confusion . . . —nothing is more dangerous, madam, than a wish coming sideways in this unexpected manner upon a man . . ." Worse yet, what Tristram wishes is of course a riddle, and that stated in the most equivocal manner. "I wish either my father or my mother, *or* indeed both of them, . . . had minded what they were about when they begot me" [1.1.4; italics mine]. *Both* mother and father have some mole of nature. The reason rendered is another riddle. The vocabulary, furthermore, conveys nothing but uncertainty: wish, either . . . or, had they, considered, possibly, perhaps, for aught they knew, even, might, persuaded, likely. Nevertheless, though the whole sense hangs on such doubtful supports, the sentence structure is quite formal and consciously wrought: the repetition of phrases in parallel form, "had minded," "had they duly considered," "had they duly weighed," "that not only, but that"; parallel clauses; general statement (had they . . . then doing) and division; periodic and climactic construction. Thus the technique of equivocation and doubt expressed within formal structures is established from the outset. If this is whimsy, it is the most calculated whimsy in English literature.

This first sentence, so calculated to break down the floodgates of the brain and let Curiosity with her damsels swim in, is punctuated by the second, one of the figures of "communication" (deliberating with the audience) by which Sterne conducts his arguments, as we have seen, both in his sermons and in *Tristram*. Every answer asks a new, hitherto undiscovered, question. Finally the chapter ends, having run through one page but a dozen complications, with another of Sterne's characteristic rhetorical devices, the figure "prosopopoeia." Here the rhetorician shifts character, speaks as mother, father, reader without transition, properly, for prosopopoeia is an even bolder figure than exclamation, says Cicero.[3] "Pray, what was your father saying?" This is the reader's first introduction to his own voice. It is an important one in the rhetorical dialectic of the volume. But for his pains in acting as a figure of prosopopoeia even before the end of the first chapter, the reader gets only a final enigma, which plants a new suspicion. And for the first time he has to deal with his own bawdy. The chapter opens with Tristram the wistful wisher, proceeds to his communication with the audience, to his role as instructor (in the Lockean terminology of the animal spirits rutted in a mad path), changes to a dialogue between mother and father Shandy, introduces the reader asking a question, and ends with Tristram (in new character) provoking the reader's most deplorable thoughts.

The reader continues his questioning: "Then, positively, there is nothing in the question, that I can see, either good or bad." But a note of doubt has come into his own voice, he should notice: positively— that I can see. But the doubt permits more explanation and the riddle is unwinding, as poetic and symbolic riddles do not. The play on epithets for the word "question" is a guide to the approaching resolution: is it "a *silly* question," *"good or bad,"* or an *"unseasonable,"* question? Always Sterne's complications are a formal matter, but the form must be, as it is here, brought into consciousness; once made conscious the form serves us as a map of thought. The Ciceronian structure of the next sentence, "The Homunculus, Sir, etc.," the inflated manner of the serene pedant, contains we find one of those earthy Rabelaisian catalogues, usually grotesque, which Sterne made a part of his own style. When we are told of the Homunculus (in this case, the sperm at the point of conception) as endowed with skin, hair, fat, flesh, veins, and the like, the appeal is obviously not to our visual sense, but, as with all grotesque detail, to ideas. Once again the tone and attitude has shifted, and the relations of law, copulation, and medicine suggest the real chaos of motives that nourishes the comic spirit. The reader is presented with a distorted mirror, the better to see certain curious features of his own character.

The narrative of chapter iii is merely another suspensive technique: the final statement which obviously is coming must await the complicating picture. Although we have already heard Walter's voice in chapter i ("Good G—d! . . . Did ever woman . . . interrupt a man with such a silly question?"), we have not seen him, for if we had, we (the reader) should not have acted as the figure of prosopopoeia and asked the question we did: modesty would have forbidden it. But here in chapter iii in the domestic scene, we can watch without a blush; but not without a sigh, for here is Walter noting the symbolism of the "unaccountable obliquity" with which Tristram sets up his top. The man who sees symbols of large concerns in every trivial event is a madman everybody recognizes, who by broad strokes of the artist's brush may be a humor character and by delicate shading may be a figure of tragedy. Walter's wail of woe with accompanying tear upon this occasion is rhetorical bombast applied to genuine pathetic, so that again the reader is puzzled by contrast, again he must deal with an equivocation. This is the last one, it seems, to be hung on Tristram's original riddle, for the next chapter returns overtly to the reader and his quivering sensibilities. It is only out of compassion for the reader, Tristram says, that he has begun his tale, in opposition to Horace, *ab ovo;* the reader wants to know *everything*—that is, the reader who is curious and inquisitive; the rest may wait awhile outside. "——Shut the door.——" Here is the climax to all the foolery started in the opening words. The swelling act has exhausted itself, but only one truth is told: the human mind must make every possible association of ideas to *know* any "fact." This point is the final end of Sterne's rhetoric. However, though we have come to one statement of this end, Tristram's invitation begins the pattern all over again, the rhythm of the repetitive form is beginning to impress the reader. But the conception is dynamic, still evolving, never merely repetitive. Locke is invoked to explain the occasion of Tristram's curious begetting. Philosophy! Walter begins to acquire great complication in himself. "But this by the bye." And the chapter goes off with the figure "sermocinatio," a type of prosopopoeia by which the speaker answers questions asked by a feigned interrogator. The question itself is interesting as an example of the kind of mental hopscotching in which Sterne is training the reader. "But pray, sir, what was your father doing all December, January, and February?" Madam the reader could only ask this question if she had jumped attentively through a half dozen insinuations.

Chapter v provides another sort of contrast; now a sinuous sentence structure, rising and falling, hyperbole and diminution. An opening hyperbolic description of this dirty and vile planet is followed by a thersitical swipe at the dignity of public preferment (this is not a loose end; it is developed again in chapter viii as part of the apology for Hobby-Horses). But this malignity is taken off by the self-incrimination of the cracker-barrel philosophy: "Every man will speak of the fair as his own market has gone in it." But,—*(fortissimo)* in fact he *has* been the Sport of Fortune;—however,—*(piano)* it must be admitted she has dealt no signal evil, just pitiful misadventures proper for a small Hero. This is the spirit of Cervantes. Sterne was trying a dangerous thing in working this conjunction of memories of Rabelais, Cervantes, and Erasmus.

Again the narrative is interrupted, this time (chapter vi) for an ethical proof, that is, an appeal to the audience from the character of the speaker. We have just left the speaker in the character of small HERO plagued by pitiful cross-accidents; now he tells us, "I have undertaken, you see, to write not only my life, but my opinions also; hoping and expecting that your knowledge of my character . . . by the one, would give you a better relish for the other." Ignoring the devices of comedy and rhetoric, most commentators on *Tristram Shandy* have noted this as one of the jests of the book; one says, for example, "In spite of the title the book gives us very little of the life and nothing of the opinions of the nominal hero."[4] And yet in chapter vi of Volume I we have already had a dozen or more opinions. In this chapter, he explicitly establishes his character as a rhetorician by the ethical proof. Nothing that touches him is thought trifling, because by trifles the reader shall know him: " . . . if I should seem now and then to trifle upon the road,—or should sometimes put on a fool's cap with a bell to it . . . —don't fly off,—but rather courteously give me credit for a little more wisdom than appears upon my outside; . . . either laugh with me, or at me, or in short, do any thing,—only keep your temper." This is the character of Erasmus' Folly, changing masks, shifting its ground, playing the monk, uttering bitter words with a simpleton's smile, uttering serious ones with pedantic bombast—in short, giving the world's tricks back to it. "Let no one expect," says Folly, "that, after the manner of . . . ordinary orators, I shall expound myself by definition, much less divide myself."[5] Both Folly and Tristram have in common the office of rhetorician. Folly's remarks of course are in the form of an oration, and like Tristram she knows how to confound the reader and then remind him of his befuddlement. Like Tristram, she breaks the rules by giving to her trickery the formality and solemnity of rhetorical structure. In the introductory essay to his translation of *The Praise of Folly,* Hoyt Hudson writes: "She takes special advantage of the fact that some words have two or more meanings; and when they do not have two meanings, in the stricter sense, they have two or more sets of connotations, and Folly knows how to skip among these, cutting across lots and leaving heads in a whirl. 'There's nothing either good or bad, but thinking makes it so.' Folly said it before Shakespeare, in her own way; she said that there is no truth of things, but only opinions about them. Aristotle had gravely set down in his *Rhetoric* this advice [to the same effect]." This statement would do as well for Tristram and his ethical proof in this chapter. Tristram adds one more complication to Folly's posturings: his rhetoric writes a history of the mind by becoming itself a subject of rhetoric.

In chapter viii Tristram continues his character of himself. Having just completed his defense of Hobby-Horses (chapter vii) on the same grounds that Folly would use—are not we all fools, not excepting Solomon, with running horses, drums, fiddles, cockle shells, etc.?—having completed this defense, he asks, "so long as a man rides his HOBBY-HORSE peaceably and quietly along the King's highway, and neither compels you or me to get up behind him,—pray, Sir, what have you or I to do with it?" With this tractable character he works the rhetoric in chapters viii and ix. Here he announces that he himself, the keeper of a couple of pads, cannot argue against Hobby-Horses; but then, *he* is not a wise man. Still, even Lords A, B, C, D, etc., may not all be wise, for they too seem to ride their horses. The fool first diminishes himself and then discovers that there are some "tall Personages" strangely like him. So goes the world—with one exception, viz., Your Lordship, for you are too important to play the fool, as other important people play the fool. Therefore if *you* should get up on a Hobby-Horse, I should wish all Hobby-Horses at the Devil. Therefore to the incorruptible and indispensable character of Your Lordship I dedicate this book. Chapter ix thereupon offers for sale the "untried-on" dedication to whoever *is* "Your Lordship." Thus does Sterne use the ethical proof, this establishment of his own character or characters, to conceive by refracting all obvious lights into varying colors. The techniques of foolery, irony, humor, and satire are not used to advance a logical point; they too, employed as they are to create contrasts, describe mental processes.

We have analyzed many of Sterne's methods of contrast because it is by these contrasts that he produces the objectivity that casts in relief our affections. It was not Sterne's purpose to ridicule and so diminish certain activities of men, as it often was Swift's, as in the *Examiner* and the "Drapier's Letters"; rather he wished us to consider the reality of the associations of ideas by which we make our opinions. The rights of a homunculus after all are a serious matter in Church doctrine. Locke's philosophy and Walter's type of madness are also real concerns, as are Hobby-Horses. Yet all these matters are spoken of in a humorous if not ridiculous vein. And later in the book there is the "spoiling" of the pathetic departure of Le Fever by humor at the end, a bit of bad taste so vocally resented by nineteenth-century critics. Sterne, they said, had not the sense to leave his finest stroke alone, presumably as Dickens left Little Nell's departure. Sterne's whole ability to fracture clichés and form complex conceptions depends upon the rapid shifting and oscillation of attitudes and affections. Had he allowed this oscillation to stop, he would have been either a crude satirist on one side or a maudlin sentimentalist on the other. Had he not shown a developing mental action in these associations, his book would have been clever and idly puckish, but fragmentary and powerless. He would have created no world of conception. In this short compass the world called Shandean is made up; the structure of the whole of *Tristram Shandy* can only be the realization of the forms already conceived. The main themes are already clear: communication and alienation, mask and identity, family and impotency, the world's vagrancy and small heroes' efforts to rectify it, knowledge and hobby-horses, delicacy and concupiscence, and the interpenetration of body and mind. Only the rhetorical play of Sterne's creative mind persuades us of the dramatic reality of such diverse material as an integral imitation of life.

And so the fool—begotten, haphazardly as one accident in a completely accidental world, on a lumpish woman who thinks "love keeps peace in the house" and is the type of the blind and deaf audience before whom small heroes always perform, by a man whose sensitivity has turned every chaotic natural fact into a symbol of universal patterns—introduces us to the ambiguous shadings by which science, copulation, custom, sentiment, and humors verge on one another; and we find ourselves participating in every vexed question until we are ourselves helplessly acting as figures of prosopopoeia. The charms here wound up are exactly those which find their final complete conceptualization in the last and most sustained narrative of Tristram, the star-crossed love story of Toby and the concupiscible Widow. Though the story is spread over the course of three volumes, it is developed by the same rhetoric we have just traced within the short range of the opening chapters. Now, as Sterne tells us, the story is really "one of the most compleat systems, both of the elementary and practical part of love and love-making, that ever was addressed to the world" [6.36.466]; yet the system is not in any way an exhaustive and naturalistic description. Since every event is developed and defined in the manner of Sterne's rhetoric from formal contrasts, the form of every event is a sort of synecdoche of the more intimate complex of non-Shandean love. The contrasts, in short, symbolize what is behind them in the acts of the mind. Form is again a map of habits of thinking—in this case, thinking about love. Yet the rhetorical pattern of contrasts that we have seen as fundamental to the sermons and to the opening chapters of *Tristram* is now allowed to function for long stretches without explicit statement on the part of the rhetorician. Tristram is only moderator here: he does not appear as in the first of the book as the moral commentator on *every* bit of rhetorical demonstration; for the reader has been initiated and is left more to his own intuitions. And if they be bawdy, who is to blame? The figures of rhetoric have become expanded almost beyond the province of rhetoric and into the realm of pure fiction—almost but not quite. Figures of hypotyposis (picturing) have become whole scenes; those of prosopopoeia, whole characters; those of communication, of doubting, question-asking, deliberation, the conflicts among characters. Yet the rhetorical structure shows, underneath, the constant contrasts, equivocal stimulations of the reader, and even, still, reasonably regular comments on the proceedings by Tristram.

Toby, little dreaming that his copia of military occasions is about to be bankrupted by the Peace of Utrecht, abandons himself more than ever to his fieldpieces while, at the same moment, Tristram appears to beg the reader's assistance in clearing the stage behind his uncle's back for the new scene which Fate is about to set for him [6.29.455]. And so, while Fate has Toby jingling at the end of her wires, Tristram tells the reader once again of his uncle's "singleness of heart" that makes of him a puppet so simply hinged. But he is no sooner left bobbing on the strings than the focus comes close, the strings disappear, and Toby is a human being again apologizing with rhetorical formality for his martial character: "[When I was a schoolboy] . . . did any one of you shed more tears for Hector? . . . you know, brother, I could not eat my dinner" [6.32.461]. Here he is flesh and blood, defending his reality as every human being must, Sterne seems to say, by his own rhetoric. Then suddenly he is jerked away again on the puppet wires, and we shall next see him, Tristram says, as Love's mechanic [6.35.466]. Having presented this ironic view of the enigmatic conflict between two views of life, Tristram comes forward again to tell the reader that the following narrative of Toby's love will incorporate a complete system of the world's love-making. This is to be a rhetorical explication. And as the first step in the proof, he denies his obligation "to set out with a definition of what love is." The ironic view of Toby is necessary, for the unconscious acceptance of figures of rhetoric by the reader must be subordinate to the consciousness of them; they must not become all in themselves, for they have a role as symbol. "At present, I hope I shall be sufficiently understood, in telling the reader, my uncle Toby *fell in love*." But the metaphor must be noticed. Because a man *falls* in love, is love something below the nature of man? No. Yet, gentle reader, never did "thy concupiscence covet any thing in this world, more concupiscible than widow Wadman" [6.37.469]. The gentle reader knows that love is a lofty matter, and so he is invited to paint his own picture of the Widow (on two blank pages) "as like your mistress as you can— as unlike your wife as your conscience will let you" [6.38.470]. We begin to see why a definition is impossible: the matter is not lacking in complication. The reader is to take as large a part as Toby, and the reader is no simple fellow. Already the rhetorician's contrasts are working.

Enter Walter now [6.39.472]. As a philosopher he can add one more link to the circumscription of "love." "My brother Toby," says

Mrs. Shandy," is going to be married to Mrs. Wadman." "Then he will never, quoth my father, be able to lie *diagonally* in his bed again as long as he lives." Here is a new view of love (marriage now): there are certain creature discomforts to be reckoned with. After all, marriage *does* prevent one from lying diagonally in bed. Who with membership in the marital state has not thought of it? But there is another contrast in this passage, too. We have had the close view, and now we have the ironic: all this philosophy is lost on Mrs. Shandy. This (or the?) love partner does not understand. "It was a consuming vexation to my father, that my mother never asked the meaning of a thing she did not understand."

At this point in his narrative Tristram digresses through all of Volume VII. The motto of the title page, in keeping with Sterne's theory of digressions, is *"Non enim excursus hic eius, sed opus ipsum est."* Inasmuch as the digression is a character of Tristram the rhetorician, the motto is a true one.

The story of Toby's love resumes in Volume VIII with some Rabelaisian palaver, a mock propitiation of the reader. "Bon jour!—good-morrow!— . . . but 'tis a cold morning . . . And how goes it with thy concubine—thy wife—and thy little ones o' both sides? and when did you hear from the old gentleman and lady—your sister, aunt, uncle and cousins—I hope they have got better of their colds, coughs, claps, tooth-aches, fevers, stranguries, sciaticas, swellings, and sore-eyes." [8.3.541]. This is the exordium for the new volume, in which the reader is utterly reduced to his mortal humanity, in Rabelais's way, by a catalogue of detail which symbolizes a category of thought, here the category of domestic animality. In this relation the reader is concerned in the inventions on love to follow.

The suffering party is generally the last to know anything about love, because we have a half-dozen words for the same thing. If we refuse to recognize the contrasts bound up in any one affection, how can we help ourselves, says Tristram [8.4.542]. We have already been through a dozen contrasting notions—all a part of one thing, love; and now apparently there are more to invent. (The rhetorician "invents" in the Latin signification of the word: he finds out.) Why was the Widow struck with Toby? Tristram runs through some inventions on cause, but "the whole is an equivocation" [8.6.544]. An equivocation is a sham argument accepted by rhetoricians as a device for diminution of an

argument. One does not account for love, one describes it. In Mrs.
Wadman's mind Toby got confused with her furniture. Is this the way
women think of love? Yes. Another contrasting view. Toby, it seems,
had gone down to his estate from the city so precipitously when the
idea of military adventures on the bowling green first took his fancy
that he found his house without a bed and was forced to put up with the
neighbor, Mrs. Wadman, for a night or two. If "a daughter of Eve . . .
make a man the object of her affection, when the house and all furniture
is her own . . . he gets foisted into her inventory—And then good
night" [8.8.546]. Love, then, among other things is a possession.

But this is Tristram's intellection, not the Widow's. She recognizes
that she is in love in another more conscious, immediate, and urgent
relation. She has, as a chaste widow, a certain sacred etiquette for bed-
time: her maid Bridget every night tucked in and fastened her night-
shift at the feet with a corking-pin. But if love means "possession" it
also means "freedom," freedom to plot, pursue and capture, to satisfy
and be satisfied; and when one night after Toby arrived as a guest she
impulsively kicked the pin out of Bridget's fingers, she knew she was
in love and proceeded from that point according to plan. Plan, because
love is not always a two-way proposition. The contrasts are in such a
heap at this point that Tristram once again attempts a definition, this
time an alphabetical one: love is "agitating," and so on through four-
teen letters to "ridiculous." Once more a Rabelaisian catalogue symbolizes a category of thought; and this time the category is the category
that includes all categories. Or, in another rhetorical definition, " 'tis
of such a nature, as my father once told my uncle Toby upon the close
of a long dissertation on the subject—'You can scarce,' said he, 'combine two ideas together upon it . . . without an hypallage'."

Not all the contrasts are intellectual; Sterne also liked to draw
pictures of them. Toby stands in his sentry box puffing away, planning
his campaign over the Plan of Dunkirk, when enters Mrs. Wadman,
according to her plan. Mrs. Wadman has a great stroke of generalship:
her forefinger cannot quite follow the attack as Toby with his pipe
describes it on the Plan [8.16.554]. The small "turns and indentings"
she is interested in, and Toby shifts to *his* forefinger. Here is the precise
picture: the two forefingers, traveling along parallel, now barely, barely
touching with little equivocal touches, two forefingers, two sexes, two

warring plans—in full battle a hair's breadth apart. Similarly, the Widow's Eve-eye looks out from another emblematical contrast. "I am half distracted, Captain Shandy, said Mrs. Wadman, holding up her cambrick handkerchief to her left eye, . . . —a mote—or sand—or something . . ." "There is nothing, my dear paternal uncle! but lambent delicious fire, furtively shooting out from every part of it, in all directions, into thine" [8.24.576–577]. Now this eye is a figure of rhetoric and belongs as much to Tristram the rhetorician, who is inventing his discourse on love, as to the Widow. He does not want the reader to *forget that:* "An eye is for all the world exactly like a cannon . . . I don't think the *comparison* a bad one: However, as 'tis made and placed at the head of the chapter, as much for use as *ornament,* all I desire in return, is, that whenever I speak of Mrs. Wadman's eyes . . . you keep it in your fancy" [8.25.577; italics mine]. And so there stand the man of war and the soft wooing Widow, eye to eye, the primordial contrast.

Sterne's stock of invention on this subject apparently was endless because each contrast is a contrast with every other one; he has something new to say on the same subject in almost every chapter for another volume and a half. There is the contrast between "my father's ass and my hobby-horse" [8.31.584], in which a three-valued metaphor involves humors, madness, and concupiscence. There is Walter's philosophical dissertation on two kinds of love, rational and natural, according to Plato, Ficinus, and others, which he would fulfill to ideal perfection, were he an Asiatic monarch, by obliging Toby, *nolens volens,* to beget one subject a month of the most beautiful women in the empire [8.33.586], to which opinion in his dialectical turn Toby asserts the dignity of the individual by denying that he would get a child, *nolens volens,* for any monarch, in which opinion Yorick, in his dialectical turn, moralizes that there is more sense than in all the poets and rhetoricians, whom he has read so much. There is Mrs. Shandy's opinion: "love keeps peace in the house"; and Slop's: " 'tis Virginity which fills paradise."

Then, when Toby himself discovers the delicious sentiment of love, Walter promptly discovers to Toby that love "is not so much a SENTI-MENT as a SITUATION" [8.34.589]. The Widow had first to gain her point; that accomplished, she would now require of Toby, now *in* the situation, certain formalities. Formalities, Walter knows, are complications, and he knows also that Toby will not simply march up to the Widow, declare his sentimental heart, and carry the thing off. Walter is *all* right of course. This is not a sentimental story, in the sense that a pure and good heart will carry off the honors. In fact, it is not long before, with some rhetorical demonstration (by a flourishing stick) on liberty, Trim does what "a thousand of my father's most subtle syllogisms" could not have done: he conjures up in Toby the Spirit of Calculation [9.12–13.614–617]. The Spirit, though planted at this point, does not compel Toby's undivided attention until his final disillusionment as the volume's and the book's end.

The "situation" of which Walter has warned meanwhile operates, leading to the final contrast, Toby's disillusionment, which closes the circle and is, as it were, the peroration to the whole argument. For this final thrust Tristram, in his way, discusses the rhetorical effects needed to bring it off. Two chapters discuss the way to obtain the proper wit and conceits [9.18–19.633–636]; there are two displaced, the better to allow the reader's bawdy full range [9.20–21.623–625]; in order to clear up the mystery of the two missing chapters Tristram asks the reader to give him all the help he can to "translate" the matter by a simile from Slawkenbergius [9.20–21.624]; because it "can do no hurt" an Invocation is tried, to the "gentle spirit of sweetest humour, who erst didst sit upon the easy pen of my beloved Cervantes." After all this, Mrs. Wadman is allowed to plumb the mystery of Toby's injury and Toby to get disillusioned. The whole is a satire on modesty, since modesty-and-lust is a natural and basic contrast for any rhetoric of love. Mrs. Wadman sends Bridget abroad to work on Trim to find out the real nature of Toby's injury. Trim on his side gains advantage from Bridget in setting truth aright. When truth is established, both Trim and Bridget have accomplished their aims, about which the reader is encouraged to speculate. "It was like the momentary contests in the moist eye-lids of an April morning, 'whether Bridget should laugh or cry' " [9.29.640]. And shall she laugh or cry for her mistress or for herself? Thus comes the catastrophe of the double love-drama that Tristram had promised four hundred pages earlier: "Now, my dear friend Garrick, . . . there is not a greater difference between a single-horse chair and madam Pompadour's *vis-à-vis,* than betwixt a single amour, and an amour thus nobly doubled, and going upon all four, prancing throughout a grand drama.—Sir, a simple, single, silly affair of that kind,—is quite lost in five acts . . ." [3.24.208–209]. The whole matter, we see, is as far from Cumberland's sentimental drama as it is possible to get in the same century.

At this point Sterne stopped the *Life and Opinions of Tristram Shandy;* he had written a complete system of love, as in his statement of the problem he had announced he would do, and he had successfully failed to define love, as he had said he would fail [6.36–37.466–469].

## 3. The Image of Our Mind

This was Sterne's sort of dramatic rhetoric: a fantastically involved structure of associations, every one *consciously* calculated to shift our bearings, advance on new ground, and open the mind on an undiscovered prospect. In his comic vision, love is neither ridiculous nor cynical; rather it is a social occasion which elicits all the possible roles that human beings must play in order to communicate. The sense of role in social play, the sense that everyone is on-stage, in borrowed robes, surrounded by insubstantial scenery, lies behind Sterne's dramatic rhetoric. He shows us that we create our own cause and effect by the associations of ideas which allow us to make sense of what Locke called our night of obscurity. He reminds us in his shifts of focus, in his tenuous interpenetration of pathos and bathos, in the sallies of one motive against another, that not actions, but opinions concerning actions, disturb men. Yet I have argued that Sterne's perception is of the Augustan rather than the sentimental and romantic modes, for nothing is further from his comic vision than the vague late-eighteenth-century cultural force of equalitarianism which at last refined the humor character out of existence, loved him to death. Sterne never suggests that his humor characters are really just like us when you get to know their feeling hearts better. The sense of role is always maintained; his characters remain as roles, voices, in the dialectic of our mind. They are not whole, realistic figures; they are probable aspects of human motivation. (The decline of comic, and the rise of naturalistic, fiction certainly results in part from the disappearance in the modern world of the sense of human beings as actors.) Sterne's perception is not whimsy or mere sentimental tolerance; it insists that we discover whole conceptions by understanding the *public* drama of conflicting roles. One cannot misunderstand the book in any more complete manner than to suppose that Sterne is admiring quaint private vagaries, or to suppose that the book is a texture of unconscious associations of a blithe spirit. Rhetoric must be conscious, studied, to catch men in probable public activity.

Yet in one regard, I have suggested, the book is a fantasy. Unlike Rabelais and Swift, his more complex mentors, in whose realms natural laws are suspended, Sterne allows nothing to happen in the Shandy Squiredom that could not happen in the most substantial parish in England. And yet the Shandean world of vague accidents, of jumbled time, knowledge, and motives, asks essentially the same question as Hume's philosophy: are we not living in a world where cause and effect are really a history of our mind? Is our world of ordered relations merely our fantasy? Under the comic incongruities of *Tristram* lies only the dubious. Only by understanding any occasion as a topic on which the cross-workings of accident and diverse motives may work, can we make order. This much is indubitable in Sterne's world: there are certain predictable patterns of association which can surround any occasion and make us know it. These patterns of association, with the different roles we must assume to make us realize them, are the condition of communication among men.

Viewed not as an eccentric and perverse novel, but as dramatic and comic rhetoric, verging on narrative, *Tristram Shandy* seems to have both substance and integrity. It is not fair to say, as most literary historians say, that *Tristram* turned the new novel-form upside down. Sterne created his own genre, and there is no evidence at all, either external or internal, that he had the new novel-form in mind. He did not turn the novel upside down; he did not even think of the novel. It is true that the novel and *Tristram* had one common great-grandparent, the romance (through its offshoot, the comic romance of Cervantes and Rabelais); but what *Tristram* owes to that strain goes directly to it and does not descend in the same line as the novel. Whether Sterne's book belongs in the subsequent history of the novel is another story.

Critics of course may, if they feel compelled by their own abstractions concerning the inevitability of certain novel-forms, press and screw *Tristram* into their copia of illustrations, but I have suggested that the book has a formal integrity quite its own. Sterne represents one of those artistic moments at which a total creation has been achieved. Another paradox, I suppose—that Sterne who loved and so subtly apprehended the mundane should have achieved the sublime of such absolute integrity. I would not, however, remove him from his true cultural and intellectual climate, that radical search of the eighteenth-century Augustans through the agency of satire for the true aspects of man's place in his society. Sterne, we have seen, dealt extensively with one of the main irritants of eighteenth-century rationalism, John Locke's philosophy, and was indeed the true heir of Swift and Pope, whose minds show on so many of Tristram's opinionative occasions. Satirists have been accused of every vile aberration, of course, by critics who cant about love and cannot endure the radical inspection of the ways of the world. But Sterne is already so vile in certain critical circles that I will not endanger his reputation by associating him with the most uncompromising of eighteenth-century satirists. I have not spoken primarily of his satire; but now, looking back over his forms of persuasion, can we see them as any other than the most radical techniques of the true satirist? We have noted his exploration of our habits of thought in order to turn upon us our own assumptions and reduce us to only another of the masks of the fool. He has not denied the validity of our masks (although he has not affirmed it either), but merely has enforced recognition of our role. We are a voice, a personification, just as are Toby, Walter, Slop, Elizabeth Shandy, et al. We are mock heroes, just as are Walter and Toby. And we must weep and laugh to thus discover ourselves. Yorick rides his Rosinante, Walter and Toby their pads, and we ours. Sterne has forced in every way our involvement, our ironic view of the paradox of the necessary isolation of minds and of their necessary communication. He has reduced the reader's respectability and made him understand that he is part of the race. And yet all this has Sterne achieved in his satiric techniques without denying the claims of love. We have only to remember his remarkable shifts in focus, the wide and the narrow, the far and the near, Toby now dangling, capering, absurd puppet, and Toby now a man mad as all men must be mad in the necessity of dramatizing his passions, or the reader, now pursuing an unsavory train of logic and now seeing himself trapped as all men are trapped by his typical curiosity. For an honest reader, there is no escape from Sterne's radical reduction—no escape through sentiment, private inspiration, or idio-syncratic heroics;—but the possibility of the vitality and warmth of life remains. We have only, in order to save ourselves, to recognize the satiric view, the classical view, the moral scheme in which we are all types (at least in our public shows), explicable, however complex. Such recognition makes social communication possible, and Sterne, the rhetorician, has written in truth a treatise on communication.

This discussion has tried to demonstrate something of the rhetori-cal structure of the book, both in short and extended compass, and something, too, of its persuasive purpose. In Sterne's odd mind two systems, rhetoric and Locke's philosophy, theories of belief both, came together as a matrix for his own system. One cannot, I think, appreciate that foolish system if one considers the book as mere whimsy, burlesque, and eccentricity. It may be all those things, but more funda-mentally it is persuasion. Sterne would have had to be even odder than he was, could he have forgotten so suddenly the habit of his office of preacher.

• *Notes*

# NOTES, *Chapter One*

The Shandean Comic Vision of Locke's Philosophy
(Pp. 3–28)

[1]Quoted by Wilbur L. Cross in his *Life and Times of Laurence Sterne* (new ed., Yale Univ. Press, 1925), Vol. I, p. 214.

[2]In his non-Shandean moments Sterne never directly commented on his impregnation by Locke. Proof of conception is, then, entirely synthetic. Nor, to guide the synthesis, is there anything which the critic may offer of a speculative nature from Sterne's creative writings.

In only one letter does Sterne mention Locke *(Letters of Laurence Sterne,* ed. Lewis P. Curtis [Oxford, Clarendon Press, 1935], No. 89, p. 166). This directs the bookseller Becket to send Diderot a gift of Locke's works. Since Diderot was a public admirer of Locke, this proves nothing about Sterne's taste in philosophies. On the other hand, of course, only a small number of Sterne's letters are extant, and too many of these were wrought anew by anxious hands. But from the material available it would seem that Sterne's self-consciousness did not extend to his literary debts. He seems to have bothered about them only when asked a specific question. A correspondent of Hall-Stevenson, for example, speculated that Sterne "conned" Montaigne "as much as his prayer-book." "You are right," was all the information Sterne offered to this researcher. *(Letters,* No. 67, p. 122.)

Spliced into the sermons at scattered points are some correspondences to passages in Locke's works. Lansing Hammond *(Laurence Sterne's Sermons of Mr. Yorick,* Yale Studies in English, Vol. 108 [Yale Univ. Press, 1948], p. 138) has exhibited about four pages of sentences that match in certain elements, but these matchings are often ill-fits; furthermore, as Hammond observes, eighteenth-century sermons were often a patchwork of received periods. Since Sterne's interest in the problem of reality was always mundane, the sermons are not the place to look for an intellectual motive of the sort I have sketched. After all, his rural parishioners would scarcely expect—or receive—more than a "theological flap upon the heart." And nothing can be "proved" about Sterne's thought from the sermons, because anything can be proved. For example, a central hypothesis of Locke's *Essay* is that morality can be discovered by means purely rational. But Sterne's sermon, "The Abuses of Conscience Considered," following Swift, denies the proposition. Is this a denial of Locke? Probably not, for this position may as well reflect Locke's warning in *The Reasonableness of Christianity* that reason

alone never prevails on the multitude. A sermon is not a philosophical dissertation and its ideas do not need precise logical discrimination. The preacher is
supplied an order; the artist, on the other hand, must discover his own.

The one direct comment by Sterne on Sterne and Locke is reported at second
hand, but sounds plausible enough. Dominique-Joseph Garat, a Boswell for Jean-
Baptiste Suard, tells of Suard's heavy enquiry of Sterne *(Mémoire historique sur
la vie de M. Suard, sur ses écrits, et sur le XVIII<sup>e</sup> siècle* [Paris, 1820], T. II,
p. 148). He wanted to know "quels etaient . . . les attributs naturels et acquis
de ce génie qu'on aime autant que les plus beaux, et qui leur ressemble si peu?"
The solemn response cannot be literally Sterne's but it is credible in outline:
"Sterne attribuit la première cause de ce qu'on appelait son originalité, à une
de ces organisations où prédomine le principe sacré qui forme l'âme, cette flamme
immortelle qui nourrit la vie et la dévore, qui exalte et varie subitement toutes
les sensations, et qu'on appelle *imagination, sensibilité,* suivant qu'elle représente
sous les pinceaux d'un écrivain ou des tableaux ou des passions; la seconde, à
la lecture journalière de l'ancien et du nouveau testament, livres de son goût à
la fois et de son état; la troisième, à l'étude de Locke, qu'il avait faite au sortir
de l'enfance, et qu'il refit toute sa vie; à cette philosophie que ceux qui savent
la reconnaître où elle est, et où elle dirige tout secrètement, retrouvent et sentent
dans toutes les pages, dans toutes les lignes, dans le choix de toutes les expressions;
à cette philosophie trop religieuse pour vouloir expliquer le miracle des sensations, mais qui, avec ce miracle dont elle n'a pas la témérité de demander raison
et compte à Dieu, développe tous les secrets de l'entendement, évite les erreurs,
arrive aux vérités accessibles; philosophie sainte, sans laquelle il n'y aura jamais
sur la terre ni vraie religion universelle, ni vrai morale, ni vrai puissance de
l'homme sur la nature." Let us, then, look "dans toutes les pages, dans toutes les
lignes, dans le choix de toutes les expressions."

³Traditionally, rhetorical proofs, i.e., methods of persuasion, are three:
logical, ethical, and pathetic. Today we should call this pathetic proof an appeal
to emotions, or, prejudice. The modern understanding of pathos is not necessarily involved. What is involved is a play upon certain dispositions which the
normal mind can be expected to have.

⁴See Kenneth MacLean, *John Locke and English Literature of the Eighteenth
Century* (Yale Univ. Press, 1936), pp. 119 ff.

⁵"The Brothers Shandy," *The English Comic Characters* (new ed.; New
York, Dodd, Mead, 1931), p. 156.

⁶Third Dialogue, *Three Dialogues between Hylas and Philonous.*

⁷*A Treatise concerning the Principles of Human Knowledge,* Introduction,
§14. Much of my discussion at this point derives from Albert Hofstadter's consideration of Locke's theory of communication in *Locke and Scepticism* (New
York, Albee Press, 1935), pp. 115–124.

⁸*Principles of Human Knowledge,* Introduction, § 20.

⁹The elusive narrator, his sudden shifts in tone, attitude, and topic, his similarity to Erasmus' Folly, the addresses to the reader, the subject matter, the
hyperbolic expressions, digressions, and mad logic—all these Sterne shares with
Swift. For a mighty documentation of the similarity of Sterne's manner to that

of the members of the Scriblerus Club, see James A. Work, "The Indebtedness of Laurence Sterne to Certain English Authors, 1670–1740" (unpubl. diss.; Yale, 1934).

[10]So said John Croft in his anecdotes of Sterne. Quoted in *The Works of Laurence Sterne*, ed. Wilbur L. Cross (12 vols.; Cambridge, Mass., The Jensen Society, 1906), Vol. VI, p. 13.

[11]*Letters*, No. 192, p. 319; No. 38A, p. 76; No. 185, p. 305.

[12]Matthew Prior, "Dialogue between Mr. Locke and Seigneur de Montaigne" and "Verse Intended for Locke and Montaigne," in *Dialogues of the Dead, and Other Works in Prose and Verse*, ed. A. R. Waller (Cambridge Univ. Press, 1907).

[13]Carl L. Becker, *The Heavenly City of the Eighteenth-Century Philosophers* (Yale Univ. Press, 1932), p. 68.

[14]*Aspects of the Novel* (New York, Harcourt, Brace, 1927), p. 165.

[15]*Rabelais*, Bk. III, chap. xvi.

[16]*Illustrations of Sterne* (London, 1812), Vol. II, p. 42.

[17]*The Sermons of Mr. Yorick*, Vol. II (Vol. VII of Sterne's *Works*, Shakespeare Head Edition, Oxford, 1927), p. 53.


# NOTES, *Chapter Two*

Sterne's Use of Locke in Character and Situation
     (Pp. 29–61)

[1]Isaac Watts, *Logick: or, The Right Use of Reason in the Enquiry after Truth. With a Variety of Rules to Guard against Error*. The remarks quoted are from pp. 3 and 4 of the fifth edition (London, 1733).

[2]William Duncan, *The Elements of Logick* (7th ed.; London, 1776).

[3]*Tom Jones*, Bk. 10, chap. 2.

[4]*Ibid.*, Bk. 3, chap. 3. Italics mine.

[5]*Sermons* (as cited in note 17 to chap. i), Vol. II, p. 196; *Essay concerning Human Understanding*, 4.19.

[6]The chapter on "Association of Ideas" was not added until the fourth edition, 1700.

[7]"The Time-Scheme of Tristram Shandy and a Source," *PMLA*, LI (1936), 803–820.

[8]B. H. Lehman, "Of Time, Personality, and the Author," *Studies in the Comic* (Univ. Calif. Publ. English, Vol. VIII, No. 2, 1941), pp. 239 ff. Although I here dispute Professor Lehman's interpretation of Tristram's time scheme, his criticism has seemed to me among the best and most suggestive considerations of Sterne's art.

[9]*John Locke and English Literature of the Eighteenth Century* (Yale Univ. Press, 1936), pp. 86 ff.

[10]*Essay*, 2.33. Cf. Hobbes's account of the "train of thoughts" (*Human Nature*, chap. iv; *Leviathan*, Pt. I, chap. 3). Hobbes's concern is with the connections which bring ideas together in the imagination. His discussion is roughly

similar to Locke's treatment of relation, 2.25 ff. But Locke stresses the necessity of the conscious searching out of relations, while Hobbes discusses "unguided" "trains of thoughts" as well. Hume's development of the "association of ideas" (*Human Nature*, Bks. I and II, Pt. I, § 4; *Human Understanding*, § 3) makes of it a basic principle, a natural "attraction" among ideas, established by custom, which enables us to organize the phenomenal world. Not all ideas need to be analyzed before we can act rationally (as for Locke), since we learn by customary experience. See also, *passim*, the discussions of custom and sympathy.

[11]*Op. cit.* (above, note 9 to chap. i).

[12]Wilbur L. Cross discusses Sterne's reading in his *Life and Times of Laurence Sterne*, Vol. I, pp. 127 ff.

[13]Introduction to *Joseph Andrews* (New York, Rinehart, 1948), pp. xiii–xv.

# NOTES, *Chapter Three*

Wit and Sentimentalism in the Shandean World
  (Pp. 62–75)

[1]Herbert Read has discussed Sterne's will to instruct by way of *Tristram*, in *The Sense of Glory* (Cambridge Univ. Press, 1929). The paradox of a moral Sterne, Mr. Reed argues, "will be found more acceptable when the world begins to read that neglected half of Sterne's genius—his sermons. There is no inconsistency—in style, in manner and in sincerity and aim—between his sermons and *Tristram Shandy*."

[2]*Letters* (as cited in note 2 to chap. i), No. 74, p. 134.

[3]Quoted in Cross, *Life* (as cited in note 1 to chap. i), Vol. I, p. 220.

[4]*Sermons* (as cited in note 17 to chap. i), Vol. I, p. 14.

[5]*Letters*, No. 38B, p. 79.

[6]For the eighteenth century, imagination, fancy, and invention are closely allied terms, and represent a quality always considered ingredient to wit. Faith Grigsby Norris, "Pope as the 18th Century Saw Him: A Study of the Standards by Which Alexander Pope Was Judged between 1705 and 1800" (unpubl. diss.; Univ. of California, 1947), Pt. X, § ii, traces the use of these terms in the criticism of the time.

[7]In his sermon "The Levite and His Concubine" Sterne distinguishes between the "malignity" and the "festivity" of wit: "The one is a mere quickness of apprehension, void of humanity, . . . the other . . . so pure and abstracted from persons . . . if it touches upon an indecorum, 'tis with the dexterity of true genius, which enables him rather to give a new color to the absurdity."

"[He] has a great character in these parts as a man of learning and wit," Sterne wrote of Sterne to Garrick (*Letters*, No. 45, p. 86).

[8]Wit, necessary as it is to shorten expression, to open new categories and subvert the old ones, to stop up Aeolists (as Swift used it), or merely to allow the witty to enjoy themselves, is peculiarly subject to the definitive urge. To trace in detail all the definitions handed down by seventeenth- and eighteenth-century literary arbiters brings one, slowly but surely it seems to me, to no conclusion.

It is a lexicographer's job. In works of art we must trust the context for definition. Certain distinctions can be made—true wit and false wit, rhetorical wit and the plain style, and wit and judgment,—but the concrete references for these categories vary surprisingly, as individual tastes vary. Sterne's position obviously is that wit and judgment must act together. Though he refutes Locke's opinion specifically in this matter, the context of that specific reference is much wider. Certain studies of the use of the terms "wit" and "judgment" have been made— although none is complete. A complete study would require very extensive reference to the literary documents of the age, and, indeed, though it would be wonderful, might be meaningless. The word "wit" was certainly distressingly complex by Sterne's time: as we have seen, to Sterne it meant "quickness," "ingenuity," "rationalization," "imagination," "invention," "rhetorical effectiveness," "naturalness," and the ability to express in short compass a conception. Probably Sterne would have accepted Addison's qualification of Locke's definition: that the discovery of similarities in dissimilars must be natural and give surprise. And he would also have accepted Hobbes's original critical opinion that wit without judgment is madness. The one thing he would not accept was any denigration of the social and *moral* usefulness of wit.

The following studies discuss the background of the wit-and-judgment controversy into which Sterne leapt with such obvious glee: J. E. Spingarn's introduction to his *Critical Essays of the Seventeenth Century* (Oxford, Clarendon Press, 1908–1909) emphasizes the importance of the terms "wit" and "judgment" in the critical lexicon throughout the Restoration and Neoclassical periods; W. Fraser Mitchell, in *English Pulpit Oratory from Andrews to Tillotson: A Study of Its Literary Aspects* (London, Society for Promoting Christian Knowledge, 1932), traces the tradition of rhetorical wit and the reaction from it to the plain style; J. W. Bray, in *A History of English Critical Terms*, presents many definitions. See also W. L. Ustick and H. O. Hudson, "Wit, Mixt Wit, and the Bee in Amber," Huntington Library Bulletin, VIII (1935), 103–130; George Williamson, "The Rhetorical Pattern in Neo-Classical Wit," *Mod. Philol.*, XXXIII (1935), 55–81; Maurice Johnson, *The Sin of Wit: Jonathan Swift as a Poet* (Syracuse Univ. Press, 1950); E. N. Hooker, "Pope on Wit: 'The Essay on Criticism'," in Richard Foster Jones et al., *The Seventeenth Century* (Stanford Univ. Press, 1951); and William Empson, "Wit in 'The Essay on Criticism'," *Hudson Review*, II (Winter, 1950), 559 ff.

[9]I would not suggest by this statement so extravagant an opinion as that of Thomas Jefferson, otherwise a sober man, that the "writings of Sterne form the best course of morality that ever was written." *(Writings of Thomas Jefferson,* ed. Lipscomb and Bergh [Washington, D.C., 1904], Vol. VI, p. 258.)

[10]Lecture IX, Lectures of 1818. Coleridge does not credit Sterne for this observation, although he is speaking of Sterne. T. M. Raysor, editor of *Coleridge's Miscellaneous Criticism* (London, Constable, 1936), notes that "this sentence is a paraphrase of a passage in Richter, section 32." Richter, of course, had studied Sterne. Richter's passage comes from one of Sterne's letters (No. 38A in *Letters*). Thus does criticism slowly broaden down.

[11]Doris B. Garey, "Eighteenth Century Sentimentalism" (unpubl. diss.; Univ. of Wisconsin, 1941).

[12]There is real evidence that in *A Sentimental Journey* Sterne was perpetrating a hoax to calm his critics and levy a new tax on the public. That he was dying rather rapidly, that his wife and daughter were heavy charges, and that his critical resistance was weakening as he saw the change in public feeling and its increasing demand for the stickier sort of pathetic, are matters considered in detail in a quite convincing explanation of this hoax by Rufus Putney, "The Evolution of 'A Sentimental Journey'," *Philol. Quart.*, XIX (1940), 349–369. See also W. B. C. Watkins' answer to the standard charge that Sterne was insincere and self-indulgent, in *The Perilous Balance* (Princeton, 1939).

[13]*The Letters of David Hume*, ed. J. Y. T. Grieg (2 vols.; Oxford, Clarendon Press, 1932), Vol. II, p. 269.

[14]This argument is basic to Bk. III, "Of Morals," in the *Treatise on Human Nature*, but see particularly the following references in the edition by L. A. Selby-Bigge (Oxford, Clarendon Press, 1888); pp. 318–320, 359, 365, 375, 385, 386, 576, 604.

[15]*Letters*, No. 47, p. 89.

# NOTES, *Chapter Four*

The Philosophy of Rhetoric
(Pp. 79–97)

[1]*Tristram Shandy*, 1.10.22: "But this is not the moral of my story: The thing I had in view was to shew the temper of the world in the whole of this affair"; 1.10.23: "I insist upon it that you read the two following chapters, which contain such a sketch of his life and conversation as will carry its moral along with it."

[2]*Institutes of Oratory*, trans. J. S. Watson (London, 1907), 3.7.10; 4.2.34.

[3]Inartificial proofs are those not invented, such as witness, documents, etc. Artificial proofs are those derived from reasoning.

[4]That is, testimony from the character of the speaker. The proofs of rhetoric are traditionally three: ethical, logical, and pathetic.

[5]*The English Humourists of the Eighteenth Century* (London, Macmillan, 1924), p. 168.

[6]*Literary Remains*, ed. H. N. Coleridge (4 vols.; London, 1836–1839), Vol. I, p. 141. Italics mine. Cf. Coleridge's opinion on Sterne's Cervantic humor, quoted in chap. iii, p. 72, above.

[7]The moderns whom, " 'tis strange," Walter did not know—Vossius, Skioppius, Ramus, and Farnaby—could have given him no shrewder guess at the passions and weaknesses of his respondent (in Sterne's words) than the ancients— Cicero, Quintilian, and Aristotle—whom also he did not know. Certainly postclassical literature enlarged the field of rhetoric; from oratory it was extended to prose forms and to poetry; but I hope to show that classical theory said all there was to say about the *basic* premises of rhetoric. In particular applications, of course, theory has found and will continue to find new critical insights into the function of rhetoric. But of the moderns known to Sterne as unknown to Walter —Vossius, Skioppius, Ramus, and Farnaby—this much is pertinent: all rework

the ancients and all, except Ramus, give long lists of subjects for invention and of methods for engaging the affections. Farnaby, for example, provides an index of more than two hundred commonplaces, from *abstimentia* through *uxor,* with suggested arguments for each. Only Ramus disputed Aristotle's distinction between logical and rhetorical argument, maintaining that invention of arguments belongs to logic and the use of figures to rhetoric. His contention, though prevailing and to a high degree accountable for the idea that rhetoric is meaningless ornament, vitiates Aristotle's meaning. Sterne and Walter obviously are in the Aristotelian tradition.

⁸*The Correspondence of William Cowper,* arr. Thomas Wright (London, Hodder & Stoughton, 1904), Vol. I, p. 64.

⁹Richard Blackmore's *The Accomplished Preacher: or, An Essay upon Divine Eloquence* (1731) apparently is an exception to the prevailing emphasis upon the plain style. A man may give "theological lectures" without passion, but not sermons, says Blackmore, for "without it how shall he be able to amplify, exaggerate, encourage, and persuade . . . and not give over till having touched the hearts and got within the breasts of his hearers, he triumphs over their passions and leaves them determined to follow?" But Pope's opinion was that Blackmore was a master of the bathetic rather than the pathetic, and some of the most exquisite examples in *Peri Bathous; or, The Art of Sinking in Poetry,* a mock rhetoric, are from Blackmore-in-passion. This merely proves again that rhetorical theory is not a formula for producing literature; it is a form for the imagination.

But that Blackmore's theory was old-fashioned is indicated by the publisher's preface to the reader; he apprehends some disagreement from the reader on the head of Blackmore's stress on the passions and his dislike of the plain style. For, says he, the Christian faith carries its own inexorable logic, and the Christian need not rely on the ornament of the ancients for his persuasion.

Similarly, Warburton in the Lockean tradition in the introduction to his *Doctrine of Grace* defends the New Testament against the theory that it could not be divinely inspired, since it lacks the eloquence of the Old Testament. On the contrary, says Warburton, this fact proves that the New Testament is divinely inspired because "eloquence . . . is nothing more than a persuasive . . . to gain a fair hearing; and . . . the end of eloquence is to stifle reason and inflame the passions." For a history of the plain style in homiletics see Richard F. Jones, "The Attack on Pulpit Eloquence in the Restoration," *Jour. English and Germanic Philol.,* XXX (1931), 188–217; W. Fraser Mitchell, *English Pulpit Oratory* (as cited in note 8 to chap. iii), and J. E. Spingarn, *Critical Essays of the Seventeenth Century* (Oxford, Clarendon Press, 1908–1909), Introduction.

¹⁰*The Rhetoric of Aristotle,* trans. Lane Cooper (New York, Appleton, 1932), 1.1, p. 6.

¹¹*Ibid.,* 1.2, p. 13.

¹²In the *Gorgias,* Socrates "proves" that "rhetoric is the art of persuading an ignorant multitude about the justice or injustice of a matter, without imparting any real instruction." But Everett Lee Hunt, "Plato and Aristotle on Rhetoric and Rhetorician" (in *Studies in Rhetoric and Public Speaking in Honor of James Albert Winans,* New York, Century, 1925), shows that similar later criticism completely ignores Aristotle's basic theory of rhetoric. Hunt points out that

whereas Plato sought to reform life, Aristotle was more interested in reorganizing theory about life, and that for this reason Aristotle's rhetoric is largely detached from both morality and pedagogy. It is unmoral. While Plato emphasizes truth, for Aristotle probability forms the very groundwork of rhetoric. Rhetoric is frankly an art of appearances. Realizing with Plato that a general audience cannot be instructed by close reasoning, Aristotle substitutes in rhetoric the enthymeme for the syllogism, example for induction. Aristotle in the Sophistic Elenchi analyzed and classified fallacies with the purpose of enabling the rhetoricians to use them more freely.

But Socrates' criticism became a formula for subsequent attacks on rhetoric and Cicero refers to Socrates in expressing his own theory: ". . . he separated in his discussions the ability of thinking wisely and speaking gracefully, though they are naturally united . . . Hence arose the divorce, as it were, of the tongue from the heart, a division certainly absurd, useless, and reprehensible, that one class of persons should teach us to think, and another to speak rightly." *(De Oratore,* III, 16.)

¹³Published in 1718, posthumously. The work was popular in England; a translation by William Stevenson, Glasgow, 1722, went through many editions. The quotation is from the Paris edition of 1872, pp. 14 and 15.

¹⁴*Institutes of Oratory,* 2.16.111.

¹⁵Aristotle's rhetorical theory is sometimes set in opposition to Cicero's in historical treatments of style. Morris W. Croll, for example, in his essay on " 'Attic Prose' in the Seventeenth Century," *Studies in Philology,* XVIII (1921), 79–128, sets up Aristotle as the inspiration for the reform of prose style in that period. Croll points to Aristotle's emphasis on invention of arguments on the one hand and Cicero's *schemata verborum* on the other. Furthermore, Cicero's devotion to the sophistic scheme, which conceived the individual as a sort of mirror reflecting the character and interests of his state, was, says Croll, in direct opposition to the Attic style of the later seventeenth century. But while it is true that seventeenth-century prose may reflect an anti-Ciceronianism, it does not therefore follow Aristotle. The antithesis is false. "Ciceronianism" refers to Cicero's practice in his orations, but in his theoretical discussions his emphases are much the same as Aristotle's, and like Aristotle he stresses the form of thought. *(De Inventione, Topica,* and *De Oratore.)* For all we know, had Aristotle orated, he might have been as "Ciceronian" as Cicero. The *schemata verborum* are emphasized in Cicero's theoretical work no more than in Aristotle's. And as for emotional sophistry, certainly Aristotle, who analyzes every emotion to discover premises for argument and advocates the use of the fallacies of logic *(Rhetoric,* 2.24), is as abandoned as Cicero. I labor this point because I believe that rhetorical theory must be the same in one age as in another and I have chosen to use Aristotle's incisiveness to guide this discussion of the philosophy of rhetoric.

¹⁶Published by Cambridge University Press, 1909.

¹⁷*Rhetoric* (trans. Jebb), 2.2; 2.3; 2.4; 2.8.

¹⁸*Ibid.,* 2.22.

¹⁹*Ibid.,* 1.1.

²⁰Bacon, whose rhetorical theory represents the main line of Aristotelianism, even proposed a complete store of specific and general arguments for any topic.

[21]"Essay on Rhetoric," *Works,* ed. Masson (London, 1897), Vol. X, p. 37.

[22]*Elizabethan and Metaphysical Imagery* (Chicago Univ. Press, 1947).

[23]Rabelais, Bk. II, chap. iii.

[24]"Science and English Prose Style in the Third Quarter of the Seventeenth Century," *PMLA,* XLV (1930), 977–1009; "The Attack on Pulpit Eloquence in the Restoration," *Jour. English and Germanic Philol.,* XXX (1931), 188 ff.

[25]*Studies in Philology,* XVIII (1921), 79 f.

[26]Published by Yale Univ. Press, 1941. See the Introduction and p. 13.

[27]*De Oratore,* 3.52.53.

[28]*English Institute Essays, 1948* (Columbia Univ. Press, 1949), pp. 123–152.

# NOTES, *Chapter Five*

"Tristram Shandy's" Holy Beginnings
(Pp. 98–106)

[1]*Letters* (as cited in note 2 to chap i), Appendix, no. xxix, p. 446.

[2]*Sermons* (as cited in note 1 to chap. i), Vol. II, advertisement for No. XII, p. 66.

[3]*Correspondence,* arr. Thomas Wright, Vol. I, p. 64.

[4]See Lansing Hammond, *Laurence Sterne's Sermons of Mr. Yorick* (Yale Studies in English, Vol. CVIII; Yale Univ. Press, 1948).

[5]*Letters,* No. 183, p. 301.

[6]*Tristram Shandy,* 4.6–7.276–278.

[7]*Sermons,* Vol. I, p. 14.

[8]*Ibid.,* Vol. I, p. 204.

[9]*Ibid.,* Vol. II, p. 67.

[10]*Letters,* No. 38A, p. 76.

[11]That Sterne was interested in the pulpit oratory of Dr. Slop's church is apparent from a passage in a letter to Mrs. Sterne in 1762 *(Letters,* No. 84, p. 154): "I have been three mornings together to hear a celebrated pulpit orator near me, one Pere Clement, who delights me much . . . ; most excellent . . . his manner theatrical, and greater, both in his action and delivery, than Madame Clairon, who, you must know, is the Garrick of the stage here; he has infinite variety; his pulpit . . . a stage, and the variety of his tones would make you imagine that there were no less than five or six actors on it altogether." In a note to this passage, Curtis quotes from a contemporary diary of an English preacher in Paris at the time who records with dismay that he saw Sterne very attentive to this Papist, even when he denounced English heretics.

# NOTES, *Chapter Six*

The Rhetoric of Self-Consciousness
(Pp. 107–128)

[1]To a friend he writes *(Letters* [as cited in note 2 to chap. i], No. 229, p. 411)

that for a man with a taste for humor " 'tis like reading *himself* and not the *book.*" Sterne's italics.

[2]So Aristotle, *Rhetoric,* 2.20. Aristotle also suggests the emotional effect to be gained by disputing a maxim, as Sterne does here.

[3]That is, the topics of argument, definition, division, cause and effect and consequent and antecedent, comparison, similitude, and contrary. There are the relations from which arguments start. See *Tristram Shandy,* 2.2.85.

[4]*Arte of English Poesie* (Cambridge Univ. Press, 1936), p. 171.

[5]Cf. Quintilian, 4.3.1–17.

## NOTES, *Chapter Seven*

Rhetorical Structure as Drama
    (Pp. 129–150)

[1]"Trust in God." Cf. chap. vi, p. 117, above.

[2]*Letters* (as cited in note 2 to chap. i), No. 46, p. 87.

[3]*Orator,* § 25.

[4]*Oxford Companion to English Literature.*

[5]*The Praise of Folly,* tr. Hoyt H. Hudson (Princeton Univ. Press, 1941). p. 9–10.

[6]*Ibid.,* introductory essay, p. xxiii.

- *Index*

# INDEX